THE AGE OF ASCENT

Yogi Mahajan was born in 1950 to an eminent family of court justices in India. He graduated from Faculty of Law, University of Delhi. In 1976, he had a chance meeting with a great living saint, Shri Mataji Nirmala Devi, that changed the course of his life. He has authored several books on spirituality, including *Gita Enlightened*.

THE AGE OF ASCENT

Empower Yourself by Knowing Yourself

YOGI MAHAJAN

Published by
Rupa Publications India Pvt. Ltd 2022
7/16, Ansari Road, Daryaganj
New Delhi 110002

Sales centres:
Allahabad Bengaluru Chennai
Hyderabad Jaipur Kathmandu
Kolkata Mumbai

Copyright © Yogi Mahajan 2022
Image credit: From the author's personal collection.

The views and opinions expressed in this book are the author's own and the facts are as reported by him which have been verified to the extent possible, and the publishers are not in any way liable for the same.

All rights reserved.
No part of this publication may be reproduced, transmitted, or stored in a retrieval system, in any form or by any means, electronic, mechanical, photocopying, recording or otherwise, without the prior permission of the publisher.

ISBN: 978-93-5520-534-6

10 9 8 7 6 5 4 3 2 1

The moral right of the author has been asserted.

This book is sold subject to the condition that it shall not, by way of trade or otherwise, be lent, resold, hired out, or otherwise circulated, without the publisher's prior consent, in any form of binding or cover other than that in which it is published.

*Her Holiness Shri Mataji Nirmala Devi,
the source of this knowledge.*

CONTENTS

Introduction ix

1. Seeking Ye Shall Find 1
2. The Golden Goddess 9
3. The Three Channels of Ascent 16
4. The Miniature Universe 26
5. Collectivity 33
6. The Grounding Force 38
7. The Birth of Aesthetics 46
8. Chakra of Dharma and Prosperity 53
9. The Ocean of Illusion 60
10. The Miracle Within (the Heart Centre) 71
11. The Instrument of Love 87
12. The Threshold 95
13. The Perennial Connection 109
14. Loving Vibrations 119
15. Meditation 125
16. How to Seek the Truth 134
17. Stress Busters 138
18. Green Fingers 153
19. 'Behold the Mother' 159

Epilogue 164

INTRODUCTION

The Spirit keeps beckoning me to write—the words flow from our Holy Mother, Her Holiness Shri Mataji Nirmala Devi, who gifted to the Age of Aquarius, a unique method of realizing the Truth called Sahaja Yoga.

There comes a moment in the life of every seeker where they stand separated from their ego and question themselves, where they glimpse through their conditioning and embark on the journey of the quest for their Spirit. The realization of Truth through the manifestation of the Spirit is the message of Sahaja Yoga. It is an inward journey that takes us into the hidden realms of our grassroots, and reveals their subtle condition and vital function. Thus, we observe the wondrous process of their growth, and the combinations and permutations that define our individual psyche.

The potential of attaining self-realization is our innate quality, but for its manifestation there has to be seeking and guidance. When the desire of the seeker manifests, the Mother shows the way through the love of the living process. The living process is too simple to be mentally conceptualized because through the intellect we can only analyse or create concepts, but we cannot create anything living, whereas deep in the recess of our being is a living process that does all the living work.

Unconditional love can connect us to her because it is Absolute, whereas, the intellect is relative. Unless we find the

Absolute, we live in the relative, where we cannot differentiate between Satan and saint. Amidst the chaos of the world, we may miss out the Absolute, but it exists in an undercurrent that unifies everything. It has always been there. As we feel it, it enables us to decipher the unity behind the apparent chaos of our thoughts.

It is the sweet melody that is heard in the flow of a river. Its message is an offering of its waters to the thirsty. It asks for nothing in return. Its nature is simply to flow and spontaneously meet the ocean.

Now that moment has come for the persevering seekers of many lifetimes to be fulfilled. This breakthrough has come through the living process of Sahaja Yoga. The process is spontaneous, natural, integrating and encompasses the essence of all enlightened beings.

Today, this breakthrough of collective vibratory awareness has gained momentum globally. As prophesied, it is the Maha Yoga, the force of change that the planet Pluto heralds to sort out reality from myth.

May the one who seeks within in all honestly, be fulfilled by the grace of Her Holiness Shri Mataji Nirmala Devi.

Yogi Mahajan

1

SEEKING YE SHALL FIND

Strange are the ways of seeking
Conning you into believing 'Eureka'
When all it meant
Was another lesson learnt.

—Neha Sharma, film director

The crowd cheered the winning baseball team—the captain quipped, 'You know it is unbelievable, after playing baseball for 40 years there is so much about the game I don't know.'

Well, it's no different with our game called the mind—even after a lifetime, there is so much we don't know about it! Perhaps, a great way to know something about the mind is to step outside of it. Mark Twain said something similar, 'The two most important days in your life are the day you are born and the day you find out why.'

We are, undoubtedly, still struggling to find the meaning of life, to make sense of life, to find a purpose and to bring a shape to our existence. We have a definite feeling that whatever we know is not complete. According to Shri Mataji Nirmala Devi:

> In our human awareness we have reached a particular point. To go beyond this is the modern problem we call as ultra-modern. Ultra-modern problem is how to raise our consciousness to that part where we become one with ourselves, with our spirit, otherwise you have no meaning to your life—you don't know why you exist.

The answer to why we exist may have got eclipsed in the meanderings of our emotional and mental pathways, but the urge to find our relationship with the Whole is working itself out in the unconscious of every seeker. Are we here to live like animals: take birth, eat food, bear children and then die? What is our relationship with the Whole?

However, the intensity of seeking varies from the mental state of idle curiosity to the ardent desire, which urges a Buddha to know the Self. Outwardly, it is the urge that takes a traveller to places till he reaches the place which will stop his journey. Inwardly, it can be the place of sensitivity of an artist who seeks through aesthetics, and a scientist or a scholar who seeks through the place of knowledge. Those who are not aware of their urge also seek that place. For instance, a drug addict also seeks, but he seeks the place in the dark. He is like the drunkard who rows through the night to get there, and, in the morning, he realizes that he has not moved an inch because his boat is anchored. Similarly, in life, our boat does not move forward if it is anchored to name, fame, money, power or family. We make pilgrimage to holy places, perform sacred rituals and give to charity, yet our mind continues to row in the dark because it does not know that pilgrimage is a place inside of us. Albert Einstein reflected, 'God does not play dice with the Universe'. All this is new, but not so new;

long before Einstein, Socrates revealed that God created the Universe for us to 'Know thyself'—to know that the 'self' cannot be learnt from any textbooks; it dawns spontaneously from the evolution of human awareness.

It's living things that evolve and not dead things; hence, our evolution is a living happening. The survival of our species and our varied ecosystem depends on the evolution of human awareness. Unless our awareness evolves, we cannot solve the problems of the world. So far, whatever we have achieved in our evolution is registered in our conscious mind, that is, the central nervous system. We know through our experience of the central nervous system that there are reflexes which we are unable to fathom. Our seeking has to be fulfilled in our central nervous system. But there are also influences of which we are not directly aware, as illustrated by a person touching a hot stove. An unconscious reflex action causes them to withdraw their hand even before they experience the burning sensation. It is mediated not by the mind, but by their unconscious. Of course, for the moment, we have to bear in mind that the subject of the unconscious is very young. Nonetheless, we do not seek game-changing ideas but a game-changing experience in our central nervous system.

The digital age bombards the neural pathways of the brain with a constant stream of data that stimulates the brain but fails to crack the code of our unconscious. Technological marvels are changing the way we read, but with the breathlessness of impatience, we stop reading the non-digital.

In his ceaseless search for knowledge, Socrates confessed that he was the most knowledgeable of men because he alone realized that he knew nothing. He understood one thing: whatever he had searched so far was from the mind, but the mind is always attracted towards outward happenings, and it is impossible to take it inwards—who looks outwards sleeps, who looks inward awakes.

A middle-aged man sat before a lottery machine praying, 'God, please let my number come.' He would open his eyes, stare at the machine and again close his eyes—'Please, please, God! Just once, let my number come, you don't understand what it means to my future.'

An exasperated doorman slapped his back, 'Dude, you can't operate the goddamn machine without the coins.

'When our attention gets eclipsed by one side, we are unable to see the other side. Though we learnt to pray, we forgot to put the coins in the time machine. Without the connection, how can our prayers be answered? Without drawing the attention inwards, how can the mind introduce us to ourselves? However, we cannot force our attention to go within because our attention cannot go to something that is not material. As our attention is created by the five elements—earth, water, fire, air and ether—within us, it is naturally attracted to material things. For instance, if we look at an object or a person, it starts generating thoughts inside our head. Inversely, when our attention goes outside and it is preoccupied with thoughts, then it starts seeing everything in that colour.

To draw the attention inwards, perhaps, we should learn something from nature. In a letter to his son, Abraham Lincoln unravelled the secrets of nature, 'One starts smiling with the flowers, talking to the birds, dancing with the wind. One flows with the subterranean bondage that runs through nature; that goes up the sap of a tree to ponder the eternal mystery of birds in the sky, bees in the sun, and flowers on a green hillside.'

We cannot enter within a tree from outside. We have to

become like the sap to seek within. We have tried through the brain, but mental projections only end up drying the sap. Whatever we do mentally is artificial because it is not rooted to the living process, and without any biological process how can we become the sap? Shri Mataji Nirmala Devi reveals, 'The Living Force is that which sprouts a seed. The Mother Earth sprouts a seed, the flowers become fruit. Whereas, mental projections are linear, they give us no norms that lead us nowhere; they reach a dead end and then recoil back.'

However, we cannot help but seek outwards because of the shape of the brain. The brain structure reflects the waves of energy into vertical and horizontal components. The vertical ones travel down from the left and right channels and the horizontal ones project our attention to the outside world through our senses. Thus, our brain is wired to take our attention outwards and not inwards. It leaves us disconnected from our inner self and hence, we can't see inside of ourselves. How astonishing that we should live as an outsider to our own self! But what if there is an instrument that could take our attention to the 'Me' within? What if that instrument is within us? What if we connect to it? If reality is within, why not have it?

But to connect to that inner instrument, transformation has to come in our awareness. We have to bear in mind that if Nature can transform, why can't we? Inner transformation, much like nature's changing seasons—has its own beauty, its own pace and its own rhythm, and with a little sprinkling of patience, every season can be a 'Bring it on!'

But transformation doesn't happen overnight, unless one is visiting a plastic surgeon! When we talk about reality and all things natural, slow and steady is how it goes. Yes, everything undergoes change, but it doesn't have to be unnerving.

The Self goes through many seasons of transformation—just as beautiful as Nature's. Whatever season may come, the movement of this joy is much like Nature—accepting change with grace and beauty. And as the seasons envelop and transform it, the Self exhibits nothing but the best for others to enjoy. Finally, the season of peace and liberty stands before us, a new kind of seeking takes root and makes us wonder, 'Why we are here and what is our purpose?'

The transformational experience makes it easier for us to see inside ourselves, and know our purpose and why we are here. But there is also a thought process that overcomes it, and we can't stop it. It is easier to climb Mt Everest or go to the moon than to stop thoughts. No sooner than one thought subsides, another rises. A thought rises, but as it falls, it goes into our subconscious. Over time, the accumulated thoughts in the subconscious build up an identity. For instance, if a person is given a title, they assume the title defines them, however, they cannot *become* a title or a position.

In his letter, Lincoln points at nature. But it is a paradox that we have to search so far out to find something that is so close to us. Indeed, the sap that goes up a tree also flows to all the branches. If the sap was supplied to one branch only, the tree would dry up. As Lincoln conversed with the birds, perhaps their sweet tweets told him that the forest encompasses the whole world. Imagine two birds atop a tree, facing opposite directions, each quarrelling over its perception of the world! We may have something in common with the birds in the way we see things and quarrel over them. As we follow Lincoln through the green hillsides in his letter, we cannot miss the subterranean bondage that runs through nature!

In this subterranean bondage, we flow along the unifying

power that enables us to decipher the unity behind the apparent chaos of our thoughts. It helps us to see that the game-changing ideas and thoughts do not bring transformation in our awareness. For instance, we have seen that neither those who believe in God, nor those who do not believe in Him, transform in their awareness; nor do they generate peace. Instead, like the birds atop the tree, they quarrel over ideologies. When Mahatma Gandhi conversed with Nature in South Africa, the subterranean bondage that runs through the teachings of Christ did not escape him. He enthusiastically stepped into a Church only to be directed to sit apart in the space segregated for black people!

To seek the subterranean bondage we have to heed the Sufi poet, Rumi, 'Yesterday I was clever so I wanted to change the world. Today, I am wise so I am changing myself.'

Indeed, transformation has to come in our awareness. We love new ideas. But the new is only new for a day. Thereafter, the mind jumps to the next thing. The Sufi poet, Bulleh Shah revealed the restless nature of the mind—it can't stop running. But why hanker after borrowed ideas when original ideas lie buried within our subterranean bondage? Why hanker after pieces of broken glass when the real pearl lies within? After all, to find the real pearls one has to dive into the depths of the ocean!

However, it is not too difficult to dive into the ocean. Evolution came to us through the subterranean bondage that runs through nature. It is a living process. Hence, for the completion of our evolution, there has to be a living process. The living process exists within us—it is not borrowed. In the grand evolutionary process, our awareness was raised higher than animals so that we could easily access it. For sure, it is closer to us than the blood that runs in our veins—it pulsates in the recess of our sacrum bone known since ancient times as Mother Kundalini. Hebraic scriptures call it ruach. In the Bible, it is described as tongues of fire. Because of her golden vibrations, the ancient Indian scriptures referred to her as the Golden Goddess. She has slept for many lives but fortunately now, the tide is high for her to awaken, and bless us with a game-changing experience.

But how to awaken Mother Kundalini?

We cannot awaken her through our rational mind because she does not hear its din and murmurings. However, when we flow with the subterranean bondage that runs through nature, we easily transcend the natural limits of our mind and adjust our behaviour to its flow. It has nothing to do with ritual or dogma—as we are ready for transformation, Mother Kundalini stages her own manifestation.

Having said that, we cannot flow with subterranean bondage that runs through nature till our kundalini teaches us to swim. While the flow of its current is interconnected, our inward flow is individual. It cannot be traversed by proxy, money or charity. The onus of taking the quantum leap across the mind rests upon us. Anyway, if our meditation is conducive to our kundalini rather than our ego, she rows us across spectacular valleys we never knew existed! Her sap rises in a beautiful way, and nurtures all the branches, leaves, flowers and fruits on the tree of life. Her kiss enthrals every fibre of our being, and the sun, the moon and the stars help us to transform. We don't need superpowers to transform the world—as our awareness transforms, we will see the world transforming in front of our eyes!

2

THE GOLDEN GODDESS

*The Spirit that never dies
Is called the mysterious feminine.
Although she becomes the whole universe,
Her immaculate purity is never lost.
Although she assumes countless forms,
Her true identity remains intact.*

—Lao Tzu

There is a story of treasure hunters who dug the earth because they had heard about the legends of a buried treasure. For ages, they had been misguided and had returned home with hollow expressions. A few who found the place were unable to dig through the mysterious layers of earth that had enveloped the treasure. But a group of seekers met a master who told them the secret of uncovering the layers. He also revealed to them the nature of the buried treasure that was unlike anything they knew existed—even a glimpse would give them the key to eternity.

The seekers worked through the hard layers for days. The master had revealed that it would respond to their inner state of being. So they used ice to cool the heat of their aggressive

The Golden Goddess
The kundalini is located in the sacrum bone at the base of the spine.

sun channel. As their aggression subsided, the layers of the earth began to soften and they found it easier to dig. As their hearts softened, so did the layers of the earth.

Not long after, their shovels hit a layer of ice. They knew the warmth of fire would melt the hardness of the ice away, so they lit a fire. Soon it began to warm their cold hearts, and it brought forth a love so pure that it melted the ice. Soft golden rays danced in the atmosphere. The seekers had finally reached the treasure, but the golden light came from some other source. They glanced about and noticed that each of their sacrum bone enshrined a Golden Goddess that emitted beautiful waves of eternal joy.

They realized that the hidden treasure had been with them all along, beneath the hardness of their ego and frozen conditionings!

Under the maze of rationality, our mind has developed a hard layer that has eclipsed the hidden treasures buried within us. As we dig in the wrong place, we return home empty-handed. Not just that, it widens the gulf between our mental, economic, political, scientific and technological development on one hand, and our living process on the other.

The fundamentals of our living process are self-organization, self-regeneration, germination and connectivity. Self-organization flows from the consciousness, which is innate in each cell. This generates growth, sustenance and self-protection. Self-regeneration is the inherent ability of the living cell to renew, heal, balance and recycle its structure while retaining its profile. But there is also an invisible force that connects the cells to each other and to the Whole. After all, till we discover the Golden Goddess, the kundalini, how can we know the secret of her invisible form?

The symbol of the kundalini, in western mythology.

How does a seed sprout?

How does the egg form the organism?

How does a wounded tissue regenerate?

Why does the body throw out every foreign body except the fetus?

Where does this consciousness lie?

Whereas science is the study of matter, the Golden Goddess is the *source* of matter. Her laws are beyond all dimensions, beyond time and space, cause and effect, and science. By arguing, discussing and judging, we confuse our mind, and do not allow her to fulfil her nature. And without it, she does not manifest herself. Oh no, she does not respond to the commands of the ego, intellect or the mind because she is not in our central nervous system, and therefore, not under our control.

Like the seekers of the buried treasure responded to their inner being, the Spirit responds to our inner being. As we penetrate the layers of our inner being, we come across an emotional being inside our physical being. Next, we may feel a spiritual being inside our emotional being. Finally, inside our spiritual being, we may feel a living process—the ancients called it the Golden Goddess or the kundalini. Though we cannot see her under a microscope, she rests in the sacrum bone in three-and-a-half coils and waits for the right opportunity to be awakened by a realized being. When she is awakened, she soothes us very silently and peacefully. Her nature is to love, she *wants* to love—she can never be aggressive. She can never dominate. She respects the freedom of others.

The knowledge of the kundalini is the knowledge of the roots on which we sustain ourselves. The whole instrument is called the tree of life in the Bible. Yes, the fruit is on the legendary tree of life, but we still have to reach out and pick it for ourselves. Shri Mataji reveals:

> She is your individual mother. How can she harm you? She knows everything about you and is anxiously waiting to give you your second birth. She thinks, she understands and she is the individual mother of the individual which has been born with you all the time; who knows all about you and loves you most. She is the one who is going to give you the realization. This kundalini is absolute dharma, righteousness, absolute purity, ideal-most personality, which does not tolerate any nonsense and no compromise. She is not afraid of anyone, cannot be enticed, enchanted or tempted by anything. She cannot reconcile to anything.
>
> That Goddess 'Kundalini' is verily like the very mother of the universe, as also the grandeur of the Supreme Majesty of Soul... (She looks) as if she is cast in the image of the life-breath clad in a yellow coloured cloth of gold, but just discarding it and getting exposed, or as a lamp-flame getting extinguished by a breeze of wind, or as a lightning just flashing in the sky...
>
> —Saint Jnanadeva, Jnaneshwari 6.14

It is easier to understand Saint Jnanadeva if we examine the unit of the human body—the cell. At the core of every cell is a nucleus. What distinguishes one cell from another is its nucleus. But when many cells with their many nuclei move at a certain frequency, they become one like a microfilm. Likewise, the when the strands of the kundalini's energy rise, their frequency allows us to feel the oneness with our self. However, when the kundalini rises, she tests us and finds out what sort of an ascent she's going to have. Hence, in the beginning, only a very subtle strand rises and pierces the fontanelle bone area, and we start to feel a cool breeze. But still there are other strands waiting to expand and rise. Indeed, there is no other human mechanism of such delicacy, sensitivity, understanding, strength and beauty as the kundalini.

3

THE THREE CHANNELS OF ASCENT

Everyone who is seriously involved in the pursuit of science becomes convinced that a spirit is manifest in the laws of universe—a spirit vastly superior to that of man.

—Albert Einstein

Newton gave us the Law of Gravity and Einstein gave us the Theory of Relativity. Any new invention is not the work of a singular scientist but an achievement of the collective generations of scientists. Successive generations benefit from the investments made in the memory bank by the generations before. Likewise, our digital generation reaps the harvest sown by the previous generations.

It reveals that evolution is a continuum of a chain of events. If, behind a simple machine, there has been so much effort, then what about the Homo sapiens? How could they have evolved without the working of some conscious force? How do body cells renew, heal, balance and recycle their structure while retaining their profile? How does a wounded tissue regenerate? Why does the body throw out every foreign matter except the foetus? This establishes the premise that there must exist a

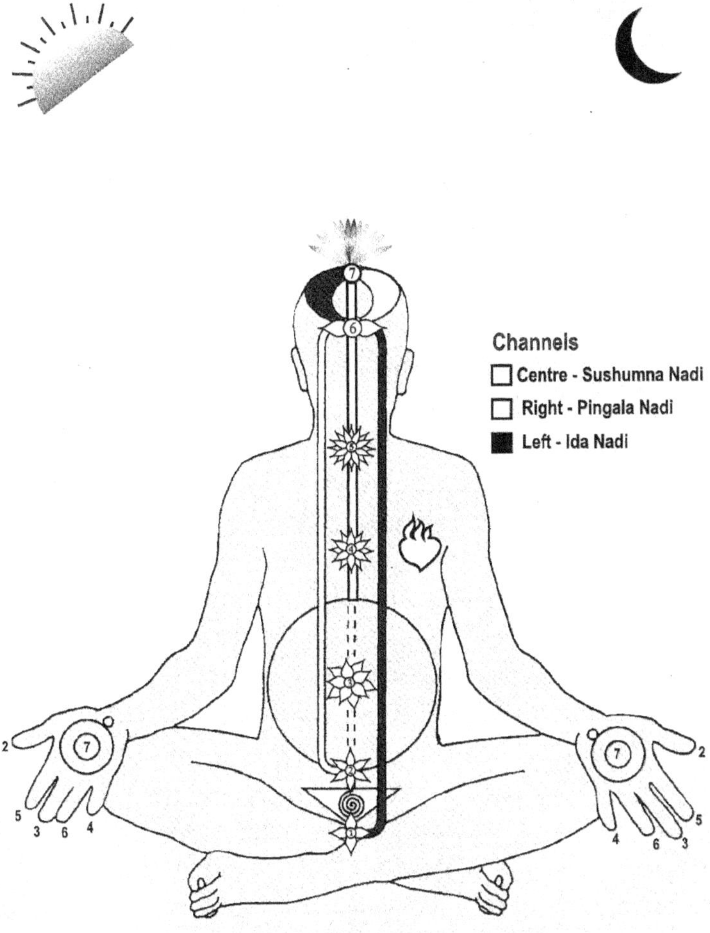

The three channels of Ascent

living process behind such wondrous events. If we see a tree, we also know there are roots supporting it.

In all humility, we must admit that we do not know the answer. We can know the advent of something that transpired in our conscious mind but cannot know of an event that occurred in the unconscious. Perhaps, some answers were found in the research of the psychologist Carl Jung. He discovered that the unconscious becomes conscious and beams information to our central nervous system. Additionally, he also said that it is possible for every individual to connect with collective consciousness.

But how, he did not reveal.

Fortunately, in 1970, Shri Mataji Nirmala Devi discovered a unique method of plugging into the mains of collective consciousness called Sahaja Yoga. We can do this through the instrument of our kundalini. New Age thinkers have also deliberated on this new awareness. It has also been described as a thoughtless awareness which results in collective consciousness. However, our situation is like that of a fish in the water—always in the water yet thirsty. There has to be a microscope to see the cells; similarly, we have to have self-realization to feel collective consciousness.

A scientist would not create anything unless he had the desire for it. The catalyst behind anything is desire. According to the Buddha, desire is the cause of unhappiness. But the desire he spoke about and the one we refer to are not the same. The desire that Buddha spoke about was the gross desire of the senses that causes unhappiness. However, there could also be the desire for enlightenment. Did he not also say that a bodhisattva, an enlightened being, in compassion, desires to help uplift the humankind? Likewise, there is also the pure desire of our kundalini to plug into the mains of collective consciousness.

According to Sahaja Yoga, in the body's physical and metaphysical fields of energy, there exists this desiring force in the left side of the body, called the moon channel or the *ida nadi*. This channel runs up the left side of the body, and brings to life our primary emotions and past memories. As long as this channel remains active, so does the human desire to survive. Thus, this channel cans our thoughts, reactions, sensations and shocks into a subconscious hard drive, wired inside the right hemisphere of our brain, called the superego. It manifests the psyche in a wider sense.

However, there must be a means to satiate the desires. To satiate its desire, the force assumes the mood for action in the right side of the body, called the sun channel or the *pingala nadi*. This is the channel of physical and intellectual capability. It develops as a by-product of its activity, the ego that gets canned in a hard drive in the left side of the brain.

Moreover, the storage space of the hard drives in the left and the right side of the brain is limited. So how do they deal with overload? Well, they simply spill over into an infrastructure outside the brain. According to Shri Mataji Nirmala Devi, the superego hard drive crosses over to an area beyond the subconscious, where all that has gone out of evolution is stored—the collective unconscious. On the other side of the spectrum, the ego hard drive crosses over to an area beyond the supraconscious—the collective supraconscious. After all, these are nothing other than areas of collective hallucination!

But another astonishing phenomenon occurs—the mechanism of the hard drives starts to function in an arbitrary manner. But that's not all! The hard drives function independently of each other, as though the ego and superego were two separate individuals. Perhaps we can understand this astonishing phenomenon if we go back to Newton's third law of motion—for every action, there is an equal and opposite reaction. Likewise, the ego and the superego react in equal and opposite directions, and thus, cause the pendulum of our attention to swing between elation and depression.

Both the left and right subtle channels express the sympathetic nervous system in the gross outside the spinal cord. Through its power of love, the living force ascends to re-establish its link with the collective consciousness. Sahaja Yoga research reveals that the activity of the living force is controlled by the manifestation of the Spirit. It forms a third channel between the moon and the sun channel called the central channel (*sushumna nadi*) or the parasympathetic nervous system. The pure desire uses its innate power of love for sustenance.

However, if the car goes too fast, we lose control and bump into the left or the right channel. If the car is bumped often, it means there is a problem with the driver's right channel. As the driver goes into action, in his ignorance, he thinks he is doing everything, though, in reality, he does only dead work. Nature does all the living work. The driver's false assumption swells his right channel like a balloon, and he becomes a dry, unfeeling personality.

Perhaps, we can better understand such a personality if we consider a sports event for physically handicapped children. A little boy stumbles during the race. When the other contestants hear his cries, they stop to help comfort him. A little girl hugs him to make him feel better. Then, all the contestants link their arms and breast the tape together. The spectators cheer for their united victory. Now, consider a second scenario of a race for kids who do not have disabilities. Parents egg their children on from the sidelines screaming, 'Come on, come on, you can beat them!' A little girl trips and falls in the heats, and the other children ignore her cries. They are wired only to win. The swelling of the ego balloon shifts our attention into the realm of the supraconscious. The supraconscious turns our intelligence blind, and that's how our intellect starts to deceive itself.

On the hand, the left channel carries our conditioning. A Zen master asked his disciple, 'Supposing you are given a choice between a tomato and lemon juice; what would you choose?'

Pat came the reply, 'Tomato juice!'

'Why?'

'As a kid I could not wait for the tomatoes to ripen in our backyard.'

It is just to say his choice was determined by his childhood conditionings. The left channel wields an incredible gravitational force of conditioning that endorses judgments, evaluations, biases and prejudices. From the amoeba to our present state of evolution, whatever we have been doing, whatever genes we have passed through, are recorded in this channel. It passes on the Yin qualities of gentleness, responsiveness, cooperation, intuition and emotions. Emotions are critical to our well-being. However, in highly emotional states, we render ourselves vulnerable to control and manipulation by others. Furthermore, the extreme edge of emotionalism may dramatically swing us into depression, lunacy, epilepsy or senile decay.

On the right side, the sun channel incorporates the male Yang qualities like analysis, competition, aggressiveness and Hatha Yoga. With Hatha Yoga, even the mind may be controlled. But a mind that is too heavily conditioned loses touch with our feelings and cannot ascend.

The parasympathetic fills the energy and the sympathetic consumes it. However, both the sympathetic and the parasympathetic nervous systems function through the central nervous system. This central channel regulates our autonomous nervous system, which looks after the heartbeat and the digestion—processes in our body that take place without our conscious will or control. As our attention moves to this channel, it stops swinging like a pendulum from the past to the future, from lethargy to overactivity, and from sadness to happiness. As the attention settles in the central channel, we experience a state of joy. Happiness and joy are two different things. Happiness is accompanied by its bedfellow—unhappiness. Whereas, joy is absolute, and hence, it does not depend on the relative state of happiness.

According to Sahaja Yoga, there are seven basic chakras. The impulse stimulus of intelligence passes from these chakras to the central nervous system through the brain cells, whereby the tissues in the rest of the body receive their intelligence. Else, how does a cell know how to go through the process of metabolism and catabolism?

Every cell is a living being and thus, has recourse to its innate intelligence through its gene. Because it is intelligent, it is living, else the moment its link to intelligence snaps, it would be dead. When a channel is overloaded, its sensitivity diminishes and thus, its stimulus is weakened. Consequently, it is unable to decode the message received from the sympathetic and parasympathetic nervous system. As the resource to its innate intelligence becomes distorted, the cells and the tissues start functioning in an arbitrary manner. A normal cell that thinks it is on its own turns into a rogue cell through the diminishing link to the body's innate intelligence. This could lead to diseases such as cancer. However, if we use the energy of the kundalini, it is possible to re-establish the cell's link to that innate intelligence.

The two hemispheres of the brain perform opposite but complementary functions. The left hemisphere, which monitors the right side of the body, specializes in linear processes such as thinking, planning, speculation and imagination. The add-on tool of imagination is also a tool to conjure abstract fear—the fear of the unknown, suspicion and anxiety.

One's personality could be dominated by either the ego or the superego or could oscillate between them. The extreme end of the ego creates a sadist and the extreme of superego creates a masochist.

The oscillation between the two channels makes us frantic. As our attention shifts from one channel to the other, our behavioural patterns change accordingly. For instance, a person may be sober in the morning, tense at noon and angry by the evening. The right-side sun channel is fuelled by the liver. Normally, the liver regulates the heating system of the sun channel but when a person gets hectic, the mercury shoots to the left lobe of the brain, and vents in the form of anger. We often say, 'He is mad at me.' In fact, it is literally true of an angry person! When the mercury shoots up, the angry person starts bellowing like a mad steam engine!

Because the moods keep changing, human nature, it appears, is in a constant state of flux, and therefore, is unpredictable. Just as each personality is different, and unfolds according to its own unique permutations and combinations;

likewise, it resonates at the collective level. For instance, there is a greater chemistry between individuals dominated by the same channel. Conversely, a left-channel-centric personality is likely to react emotionally to a right-channel intellectual and vice versa.

A common feature of these permutations and combinations is that they are not constant. They influence each other and are also influenced by other factors. For instance, influences from the subconscious easily find their way from one person to the other, much like viruses. However, neither the transmitter nor the receptor is conscious of the transmission, and nor do they have any control over it. The more sensitive a person is, the more vulnerable they are to negative influences. There is no escape, for in our state of flux, we are constantly exchanging vibrations. Just how awkward or comfortable we feel in the presence of someone depends on their vibrations. For instance, one may instantly take to a stranger or they may fail to exchange a word with a neighbour seated next to them on an eight-hour flight!

Negative vibrations are like a social virus that carries with it all the ailments of the transmitter. A person who absorbs these vibrations is likely to contract the ailments of the transmitter. It is as though the transmitter superimposes their negativity on the receptor. The transmission is so effective that the superimposed negativity latches on to the receptor like a parasite. The parasite interferes with the mental, emotional and physical faculties of the receptor like a possession. Thus, the physical, mental and emotional functioning of the individual chakras cannot be separated from the collective chakras.

The right channel ignites learning and development, and thereby facilitates creativity, behavioural patterns, and conceptual thinking, symbolic language, non-verbal conceptual art and other abstract art forms. However, their manifestation depends crucially on the delicate link with the parasympathetic nervous system. For instance, if a musician operates through the sympathetic nervous systems as opposed to the central nervous system, then his expression will be limited by his subconscious or supraconscious, and his conditioning could bounce back on the audience. Thus, the musician has to step out of the subconscious and become collectively conscious.

It follows that to keep the chakra in gear, it is important to nurture them with positive vibrations. For instance, the positive vibrations of the kundalini vitalize the chakras. As she ascends through the central channel, she throws out the negative vibrations and sucks the artist's attention back to the central channel. Inspired creativity arises spontaneously where the attention of the artist is anchored in the central channel, where he gains recourse to an infinite source of creativity. Perhaps this is from where the well-known British mathematician Roger Penrose tried to restore order with imagination and analysed the source of new knowledge. He made his analysis on the basis of strict modern mathematics and physics. He pointed that we can understand the proofs of theorems and laws, but we can only understand where new knowledge comes from if we assume that somewhere, there exists the data bank which accumulates all the information about everything in full volumes.

4

THE MINIATURE UNIVERSE

The miniature world we created with our minds and intellect has ended. Now the meaning of everything is different—our lives, our deaths, what we do between it.

—Yogi Mahajan

Ancient seers regarded the whole universe as energy condensed into material forms. New physics doesn't say anything different: matter and energy are interchangeable. Matter is nothing but energy oscillating at different velocities. Their oscillation forms the planetary system. Each celestian body such as the sun, moon, mars, etc. is a vortex or a macro-chakra that exudes its own energy field. Likewise, the earth chakra too manifests its own specific energy. As every system works through a mechanism of wheels within wheels, each macro-chakra works through a mechanism of chakras within chakras. Likewise, the various parts of the earth are different chakras that exude their own specific energy field. For instance, the earth is a macro-chakra; each part has its explicit energy field that features the characteristics of the flora, fauna and the characteristics of inhabitants of that region.

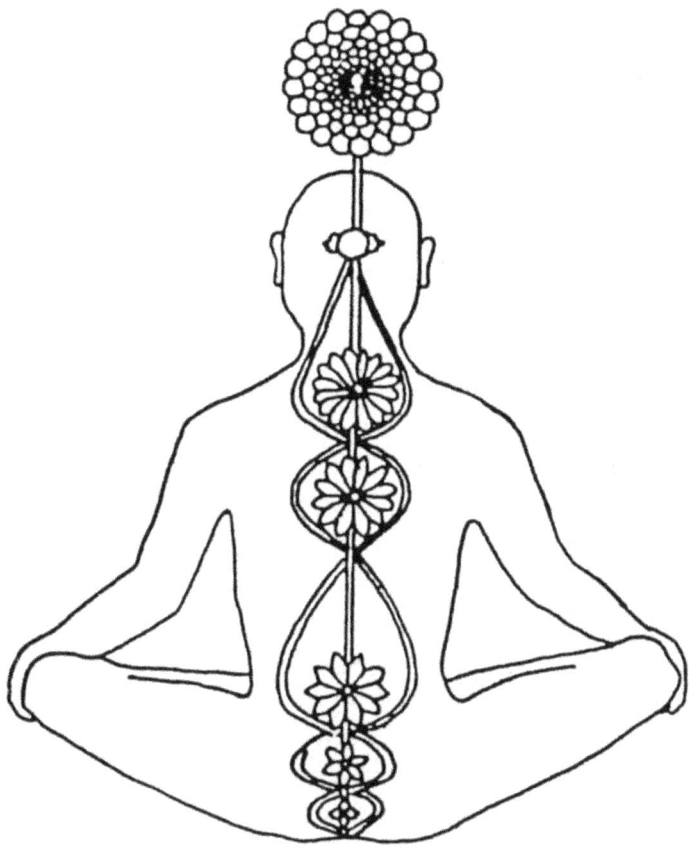

The number of petals in each of the chakras indicates their respective vibration frequecies.

Just as the planetary macro-chakras function through a system of chakras, at the micro level, the human chakra also functions through its own chakra system. Human chakras spin millions of vibrations that create a miniature universe within us. To know more about the working of this miniature universe, let us study its blueprint.

Chakras are the milestones of our evolution. As the thread of a necklace passes through every bead of the necklace, the kundalini also passes through every chakra of the human being. Our physical body has a series of nerve bundles, much like electrical junction boxes, called nerve plexuses. The kundalini has direct connection with these plexuses through chakras which lie adjacent to the nerve plexuses. The chakras feed the nerve plexuses with information and energy that keep our organs in balance and, as a result, healthy.

As the axis of each chakra is linked to our innate intelligence, each chakra has its own psyche. Furthermore, like vortexes, their clockwise spin in horizontal planes energizes the plexuses and the central nervous system. Thereby, they regulate the functions of the organs as well as the neuro-endocrinal system of the corresponding region.

As each chakra within us is the microcosm of the universe, it draws energy not only from food but also from the macro-chakras like the sun, the moon, etc. Just as the process of photosynthesis enables plants to create chlorophyll from sunlight, the human chakras absorb vitamin D from it. A stone does not respond to the moon, but our subconscious responds to it. Advanced studies reveal that the different phases of the moon affect different temperaments. And what of the earth chakra—her gravity anchors us and gives us balance. Hence, our harmonious relationship with the earth's ecosphere is intrinsic to our well-being. In 1854, the Native American leader, Chief Seattle, made the point: 'Teach your children what we have taught our children, that the Earth is our mother. Whatever befalls the earth, befalls the sons of the earth. If men spit upon the ground, they spit upon themselves.'

Unfortunately, we have forgotten to pass this lesson on to our children. As the forest fires in far-off Indonesia choked the throat chakras of millions living in the Southeast Asian mainland, it reminds us of Chief Seattle's prophecy—'Whatever befalls the earth, befalls the sons of the earth'. Thereafter, a series of world ecological summits were convened by people who were not connected within themselves or to the living process of the living earth. How could they get us anywhere? But there is no reason to give up, now that we have found the connecting point, kundalini. We have to bear in mind that if there is something so dynamic, so great, so effective and so efficient as the kundalini within us, then in all fairness, why not give it a chance? It is free, so let us keep an open mind, as a scientist does, and find out more about our kundalini and the infrastructure of our chakras.

The infrastructure of our chakras is no different from the infrastructure of the chakras of Mother Earth. What befalls one befalls the other. When our chakras spin in harmony with the earth's macro-chakras, they keep the ecology of our miniature universe in sync. But when they get disrupted by physical pollution or the mental pollution caused by the deliberations of the mind, a problem arises. Our mind is central to understanding the ecology of our chakras. Hence, to understand why they go out of gear, we have to step into the orbit of our chakras and discover how they function, how they influence our mind, and also how they are influenced by our mind. As we sow, so do we reap. Our chakras go out of gear due too much or too little of emotional, mental or physical quotients. As they respond to our thoughts, deeds, lifestyles, habits, hurts and shocks, their sensitivity becomes dull after the first few shocks of irresponsible behaviour subjected to them. Thereafter, a person can live with all the destructive ways and habits very easily. As the chakras go out of gear, the cells of the plexuses cells stop obeying their commands. It is just to say, the nerve cells stop responding to the body's innate intelligence, and hence, much like cancer cells, they start growing arbitrarily.

The chakras can also fall sick due to factors outside our conscious mind. They unconsciously absorb vibrations from friends, relatives, and the collective. Just as the body picks up the common cold from a friend, likewise our heart chakra can pick up the pain from the heart chakra of someone close. The physical proximity is not the criteria—it is the emotional attachment that is the catalyst. Not just that, a friend of a friend could also pick up the pain of the original receptor. Thus, it grows viral and manifests as a collective malady.

Conversely, a collective that has a strong heart chakra can empower the weak heart chakra of an individual. Thus, many things work out for the individual through the collective and vice versa. At a Sahaja Yoga workshop it was observed that when the block in the heart chakra of a receptor started releasing, it resonated throughout the collective, and all those who suffered from the identical chakra block found that it had cleared out simultaneously. However, if the receptor does not attend to the block in a timely way, his block would remain frozen in time along with the block of his collective.

The kundalini struggles to cross the blocks in the six

chakras before she establishes herself at the seventh chakra atop the head. Her task is not easy if the chakras are sick. She tries to repair the sick chakras, but if the higher chakras are constricted due to tensions, only a few of her strands pierce through. She uncoils and attempts to rise in her complete manifestation and does force her way upwards up to a point, but she does not follow any time frame. At the Sahaja Yoga workshops, one can witness with naked eyes the kundalini pulsating at the points where the chakras are blocked.

Where the chakras are not under strain or exhausted of their energies, they can easily be pierced directly in their centres by the kundalini. Thereafter, she enlivens the sick chakras and the deadened psyche. She doesn't talk—she works, as that is her character. She works through the subtle infrastructure of the sympathetic and parasympathetic nervous systems to energize our mental, emotional, physical and spiritual being. Thereon, the healthy chakras have a nurturing, regulating and correcting effect on the glands and bodily processes they control. Besides, they are also empowered to nip tensions in the bud.

Both the sympathetic and parasympathetic nervous systems act on the plexuses, but in opposition to each other, i.e. the parasympathetic relaxes the plexuses but the sympathetic squeezes the energy by constricting them. One fills in the vitality, and the other consumes it. At the navel, there is a gap in the parasympathetic nervous system. This is the hurdle that has rendered all our seeking fruitless so far. It is like three ladders, two of them touching the ground while the central one is hanging in the air. So whenever we try to rise in our consciousness, we move on to the sympathetic system. In death, the kundalini leaves the body; carrying the contents of the chakras and the karmas of the past as well as previous lives.

After all, we do not have to wait for death to usher us into the kingdom of heaven! Our chakras are the soundtrack of the kundalini's music. Her ascent produces harmonious notes, but if it is hampered by the negativity of fear, jealousy or hate, the soundtrack produces jarring notes. The jarring notes can be as unbearable as the suffering of hell on earth.

It evinces that, to keep our soundtrack clear, we must fine-tune the chakras. We believe that our thinking is done by the mind, but all our organs do not act according to the mind. They respond to the macro-chakras that help our chakras to nurture the plexuses with the living process. We are not stuff that abides individually, but patterns that converge in collective chakras. The merging of human attention into the collective chakras manifests a new state of consciousness—collective consciousness. The kundalini triggers the unification of human attention with collective consciousness.

Moreover, as the kundalini has access to all the passwords, she opens our inbox. It allows us to take stock of what's going on in our chakras, and, in the process, also gain access to the inboxes of others. And that enables us not only to fix our chakras, but also the chakras of others as if they were our own. Thus, as our chakras become peaceful, the macro-chakras of our planet also become peaceful—as we are, so the world will be!

5

COLLECTIVITY

You cannot have a party on your own,
You have to celebrate with others.

—Yogi Mahajan

There were three men—mute, blind and deaf. They spent their days bemoaning their misfortunes. They wallowed in self-pity, each trying to outdo the other on his misfortune. One day, a wise man suggested to them, 'Why don't you pool in your resources? Let the blind see with the eyes of the mute, the mute speak through the deaf, and the deaf hear through the blind.' They followed his advice and forgot their woes. When they pooled their resources, a collective force emerged, which enabled each one to enjoy in the other what was missing in them individually. They got together like a bunch of flowers and enjoyed the collective fragrance. As our kundalinis pool together, we form a collective force that showers joy upon all humankind.

Similarly, as we enjoy a close-knit relationship with Nature, we obtain an extraordinary power of understanding her. It allows us to see ourselves within her, and to witness an organism in which close cooperation and coordination exist among the different species. For instance, bees and ants act almost like the cells of a complex organism with a collective intelligence far superior than that of its individual members. There is no rivalry among them, but rather, relationships nesting within other relationships. Our evolutionary process was no different—life did not evolve on earth by competition but by mutual cooperation. As a cell does not grow for itself but for the whole body, it follows that deep inside, we are a collective. Hence, as the frequency of the vibrations synchronizes, they appear like a microfilm and that makes it easier for us to enjoy the collectivity of the miniature universe inside of us.

Cutting-edge research no longer views the cosmos as isolated building blocks, but rather as a network of interdependent relationships between the various parts of a unified whole. Henry Stapp of the University of California states, 'An elementary particle is not an independently existing un-analysable entity. It is, in essence, a sect of relationships that reach outward to other things.'

Living organisms are open systems. Their survival depends on interaction with the environment, which itself is a living process. Thus, our ecosystem is an interdependent network constantly interacting at all its levels. It is, thus, evident that this dynamic functions at all levels of the universe structure—from subatomic particles to galaxies, from bacteria to human beings. This further sheds light on our close relationship to each other through cosmic transaction and interdependence.

The relationship integrates both the individual human mind and the earth mind into the whole planetary mind. This, in turn, integrates into a collective or a cosmic mind. The vibration that carries our influence into the environment also brings back information from the collective mind, and thus, we are influenced by it. Not just that, each individual mind is not only influenced by the collective mind but also influences it.

This indicates that our biological, mental, emotional and cultural ties cannot be separated from the collective mind. This is verified by Sahaja Yoga collective meditations. Often, the individual catch (problem) is dissolved by the force of the collective kundalinis. A seeker may meditate alone, yet he is uplifted to a place beyond his mind by the collective power of vibrations generated by the collective kundalinis. It evinces that there is a joyful collective place where we all belong, and that we do not really belong to the individual being that we think we are.

After all, an organism that thinks only in terms of its own survival will invariably destroy its environment and, eventually, itself. The unit of survival then is not just an individual, but rather a collective pattern adopted by an organism in its interactions with its environment. What survives is the organism-in-its-environment, i.e. collectivity.

US President Franklin D. Roosevelt rightly pointed, 'Poverty anywhere is a threat to prosperity everywhere.'

Shri Mataji Nirmala Devi said it all, 'Poverty is of the mind. If a person has a mind which is sickening, he may be a millionaire—still, he will be crying. By going to the roots of poverty, by understanding why there is poverty, and why human beings behave like this, you can transform the whole thing.'

It is remarkable how global communication has awakened the concern of collectivity. More recently, a school sports team were marooned in Tham Luang Nang Non cave in Thailand. They were trapped by rising flood waters. While Thai authorities struggled to rescue them, people of all nationalities and cultures around the world watched and prayed for their safety in their own way.

At a deeply fundamental level, we are innately collective. Einstein discovered that under certain conditions of extreme cold, subatomic particles called bosons become indistinguishable from each other. They merge into one another and lose their identity completely. However, he stipulated, 'In effect, this can happen, but only at ridiculously cold temperatures, ones so low they can exist only in the mind of God!'

On 5 June 1995, those ridiculously low temperatures were reached, not in the mind of God, but in the Joint Institute for Laboratory Astrophysics operated by the University of Colorado. The state of matter now known as the Bose–Einstein condensate unravelled that material things, from atoms to planets, have wavelengths so short, they behave like particles with clear boundaries, locations and motions, but the warmest, fastest atoms begin evaporating.

The key to that transition is growth of the particle's wavelength until they overlap, which takes place as the matter is supercooled. Clouds of atoms become so frigid that they lose individuality and merge. They are not just *like* another, but they actually *are* one another. For instance, imagine a carton of a dozen eggs in which all the eggs suddenly overlap in the same slot but do not break or interfere with each other.

The discovery of the Bose–Einstein condensate helps to simply understand how the individual human mind integrates with the collective mind or inversely, from its very inception, they are the reflection of the same 'Whole'. Therefore, both the individual mind and the collective mind interact with each other and affect each other. It is indeed remarkable that groups of people, societies and cultures have a collective mind, and therefore, also possess a collective consciousness. Jung assumed that the collective mind or collective psyche also included the collective unconscious. We are not stuff that abides individually, but patterns that converge in collective consciousness. As individuals, we are involved in these collective patterns and, to some extent, also define them.

Let us examine in the next chapter, how.

6

THE GROUNDING FORCE

*At the beginning of time, the great Earth Mother
gave life to all things.
She is the original power from whom both humans and
animals increase and grow.*

—Mythology of Uluru, Australia

Native Australian aborigines regard the earth as a living organism and worshipped her as their nurturing mother. As long as she was looked upon as a symbol of fertility, she was held sacred and alive. It was unthinkable to exploit her.

When astronauts were able to look at the earth from outer space, they suddenly became aware of this intimate relationship. Their perception of her beauty and vitality was such a traumatic experience that it integrated the relationship of their individual mind with the earth mind. Needless to add, many primitive tribes and traditional collectives, both in the West and the East, not only enjoy an integrated relationship with the earth mind but also with the cosmic mind.

Advanced research has led the chemist James Lovelock and the microbiologist Lynn Margulis to regard the planet as a whole single living organism. Observations of its environmental

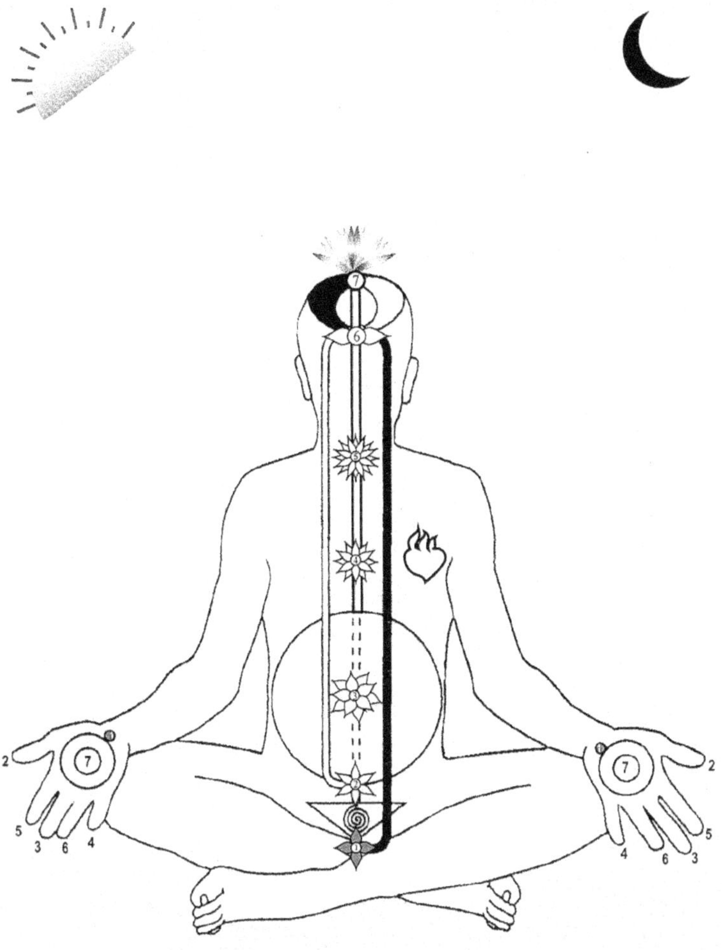

Mooladhar Chakra

properties such as the atmospheric composition, the salt content of the sea and the distribution of trace elements among plants and animals, show that intricate cooperative networks that manifest the properties of living, self-organizing systems, also regulate them.

Their discovery was not unknown to the Indo-Aryan race in 5,000 BC when they inscribed it in a beautiful hymn in the Atharva Veda:

> [T]he earth whose immortal heart covered with truth is in the highest firmament—let that earth assign to us brilliancy, strength...let her sprinkle [us] with splendour...earth is mother, I am earth's son...
>
> —Atharva Veda 1.8–9 and 1.12

However, the son cannot learn the properties and activities of his mother from the sum of her body parts, as every one of her tissues is linked to every other tissue, and all of them are mutually interdependent. Her many pathways of communication are highly complex and non-linear—her form has evolved over billions of years and continues to evolve. Recognizing that this was renaissance of a powerful ancient myth, Lovelock and Margulis named it the Gaia Hypothesis, after the Greek Goddess of the earth.

The Indo-Aryans perceived the earth as a living organism long before the Greeks named her Gaia. Her power of gravity was felt as the love that nurtured microbes, plants and animals. Each part of the earth-organism was felt as a vital organ emanating a positive vibrational field. If this area was disrupted, it could cause the entire earth to malfunction in a way similar to the human body when the chakras inside it are disrupted.

Every living process has a mind. Since the earth chakra is a living organism, then she, too, must be mindful like her sons and daughters. Similarly, she has her own kundalini that thinks, regulates, understands and heals the chakras. We can see in nature how every tree has its own limitation, how every fruit is produced in a particular tree.

The first chakra is the son of Mother Earth. It is located slightly outside the spine to guard the innocence of Mother Kundalini, who rests in the sacrum bone in the spine against the wrongful entry of unholy intentions.

In the first step of evolution, a single-cell organism was formed, like an amoeba. Thereafter, it became more and more complex and developed into a multi-cellular organism. Thus, the first chakra is the beginning of life, and as its magnetic property of innocence is ignited, one gains access to an inbuilt GPS we had forgotten existed. The GPS stationed in this chakra gives the sense of direction to all the chakras above. Just as innocence is the innate quality of all living beings, it also is the quality of the first chakra, and bestows it with guidance and protection. For instance, when an alien particle tries to penetrate into our body, the vibrations of the Mooladhara Chakra's innocence alerts the body's immune system at the heart chakra (located behind the sternum bone parallel to the heart) which then plunges into action. Despite being constantly attacked, the Mooladhara Chakra's innate quality of innocence cannot be vanquished. The cleaner the mirror, the better the reflection! If, knowingly or unknowingly, we go against our living process, its vibration sounds an alarm and we feel the hot vibrations on the palms of our hands. If we turn a deaf ear, then after a few shocks, it settles as guilt in our subconscious. Likewise, when the insulted innocence of a woman is too much to bear, she gets traumatized.

As we get familiar with the position of the first chakra within us, it becomes easier to understand the role of sex in terms of evolution. According to the theory of Sigmund Freud, repressed sex creates problems in the human psyche. However, he carried his one-sided theory too far where the spokesmen for sex have gone to the extent of advocating indiscriminate indulgence in sex. They expound the theory that sex indulgence is the key to happiness. However, sex addiction sucks the attention to the subconscious and thereon, to the collective subconscious where one fantasizes about sex. These fantasies fuel perversion like pornography, etc. Perversions cannot give satisfaction, only reality can be satiated. For instance, the more one indulges in alcohol, the more one hankers for it. A drunkard knows that drinking excessively may burn out his liver, yet he does not give up. Likewise, perversions do not give fulfilment, on the contrary, they give rise to a teasing obsession. When the famous Urdu poet Mirza Ghalib aged, he composed a couplet expressing the frustration of carnal desire:

> Though I cannot lift my hands any more,
> my legs have given way.
> But passion still surges in my eyes.
> Let there be women and wine before me.

Nor is sex abstinence or an ascetic lifestyle an answer.

> There is nothing to renounce
> There is no need to become an ascetic
> Chastity depends on the existence of lust

> When there is no lust, there is nothing to suppress.
> O Peacock, do not tear out thy feather,
> But wear thy pride from them.

It is not natural to think of sex all the time. If the thought of sex festers in the mind, it becomes a mental activity and can be used for ego purposes. Often, such people become victims of the supraconscious and get obsessed with exposing their bodies in various ways. How can sex be rationalized? After all, it is an absolutely normal and natural human desire, but it is to be understood in its proper perspective. The sex act has never played any role in human ascent. So the new ventures in sex are not going to lead us into a higher state of awareness. If sex, at the human level, is not understood in relation to man's achievement as a human being, and not as an animal, then we fail to reach the right conclusion. For example, human beings are evolved and have a sense of dirt, filth and untidiness, but animals are not aware of it. The awareness of laws that govern us also comes from the evolved state of our sustenance (dharma). We know that a balanced life is very important and that unlike animals, we have the freedom to go to any absurd extremes.

The other important point is that our behaviour always seeks the collective sanction. Marriage has the collective sanction of the society, and comes with the security essences for the proper growth of the partners and the progenies. Sex has its place in human life as the most sublime physical expression of love within marriage. In a marriage, sex leads to the growth of the relationship and the deepening of the love between the partners. They find satisfaction in this sincere, long-term relationship that ripens into a joyous family life. A joyous family unit is the nucleus for building a joyous society; whereas, transitory relationships may be super exciting to begin with, as they inevitably end, they scar the psyche. Without security, the pendulum of our moon channel continues to swing unabated for 'something missing'. But that 'something missing' goes on to elude us because we are looking for a dark cat in a dark room that does not exist! But if we look for purity in others, we won't love someone today and hate them the next day.

Occult practices like Tantrism describe the kundalini as a sexual energy, asserting that by reversing the sexual energy, the kundalini can be awakened. The kundalini is placed above the first chakra, which oversees the function of excretion and reproduction. Hence, the kundalini cannot be awakened by a chakra placed beneath it. She can only be awakened by a realized soul. Any other attempt to awaken it will result in turbulence. Sex cannot be used as an instrument of spirituality because the ascent of the kundalini is spontaneous. The test of any spiritual practice is whether it sustains the attention in the central channel. Without innocence, it is not possible to sustain the attention in the central channel.

As shooting sprees by school kids have become frequent in certain parts of the world, we must look deeper into their anatomy. A common factor that emerges in all of these incidents is that these kids have grown up in a society that does not sustain innocence, and hence, the kids identify more with the anti-hero loathed by society. For instance, the 16-year-old who went on a shooting spree in a pre-school had been sexually abused. Additionally, crime statistics reveal that sexual crimes have claimed more lives than terror.

The occult practice of calling dead spirits also eclipses the attention from the central channel. Mesmerism, hypnotism, parapsychology, extrasensory perception (ESP) and trance are all manifestations of the spirits of the dead. Likewise, animals and plants that have become extinct go into the collective subconscious. According to Shri Mataji Nirmala Devi:

> All viruses are dead plants or dead animals, that are microscopic which have gone out of circulation of evolution. They reside in the area of collective subconscious. Doctors have reached certain understanding that they are Protein 53 and Protein 58 which trigger cancer. Also, they say that cancer is caused when a person goes into a shock and the attack comes from the left in the area which was built within us since creation. This is the same area as the collective subconscious where everything that is dead is stored. So there are humans who have dead hanging around there.

It evinces that shocks and tensions in the first chakra trigger the movement of our attention to the collective subconscious, where we become vulnerable to diseases like cancer. A fragile society is unable to weather its storm. Thus, a future cancer-free society has to be anchored on the bedrock of innocence. The quality of innocence is never lost because innocence is intrinsic to the whole creation, and what is innate cannot be destroyed. It may be obscured by clouds, but after the kundalini rises, she restores our innocence beautifully, and guides us towards what is to be done and away from what is not to be done. Her intuitive wisdom gives us the discrimination to discard what has to be discarded and evolve what is to be evolved.

7

THE BIRTH OF AESTHETICS

The seeker questions the flower, 'Why does the bee not frequent you, despite your sweet fragrance?'
The flower replies, 'Sweetness is only shared with those who become one's own. Why waste it on passersby. The bee hovers from flower to flower, stealing all the nectar but embraces none.'

—Yogi Mahajan

In the desire to manifest its love, the living process expressed its joy in various beautiful forms. Likewise, the human desire for shelter led to creating a home. As its sense of aesthetics developed, humans added grace and beauty that evolved into the science of architecture. The scientific brain that captures innovations and original inventions about matter receive their impulses from the second chakra called Swadishthan chakra.

This chakra nourishes our attention whereby we can imagine, forecast and conceive an image or an idea beyond the faculty of our five senses, and thus, give voice to the abstract. In the evolutionary breakthrough, only human beings gained the add-on ability of the abstract. No animal has this ability

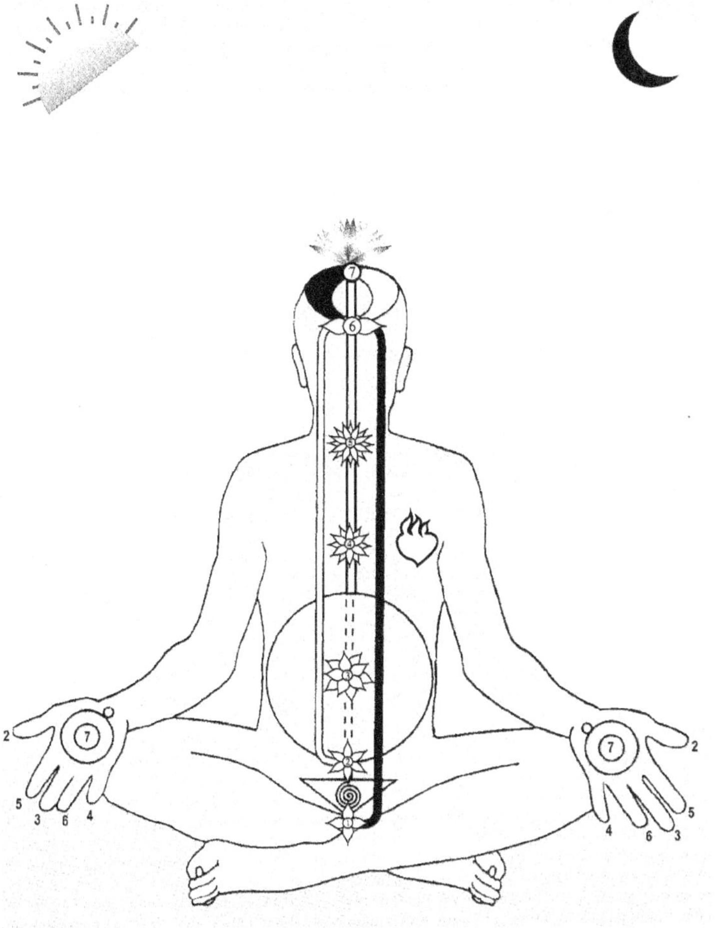

Swadishthan Chakra

because it was given to us to inquire into the meaning of our existence—to know the self.

So far, we have succeeded in using this capacity to project beyond the mind. For instance, a dramatist uses light effects to set a mood, and a musician uses sound effects to enhance his melody. The artist who uses this capacity to draw from the unconscious not only projects its joy but opens a window for others—be it a painting, music, sculpture, literature or architecture. For instance, the success of a realized dancer lies not in mesmerizing the audience but in her ability to shift their attention from their emotional and mental pressures to the joy of their inner self. The efficacy of that ability rests not in her skill but rather in the awareness of her inner self.

However, an artist who wants only to be rich continues to be poor in their work because they will have nothing but money. When an artist chases success, they drain the energy of the second chakra. The chakra provides power for creativity and thinking. Ceaseless thinking exhausts the sun channel and swells the ego. This pushes the superego down, and thus, severs the connection with the central channel, nurtured by the living process. The brain loses its elasticity and becomes like a rock. Thus, artists, planners and people who think too much, multitask, fast-track or are workaholics have a deficit second chakra. However, after the kundalini awakens the chakra, it resumes its normal shape, behaviour and condition. Thereafter, we realize that real joy comes not from creating things but by resurrecting them with the vibrations of the living process, just as Leonardo da Vinci resurrected the love of the Spirit in the smile of the Mona Lisa. All great art has vibrations that have been sustained by time.

The quality of the left side of this chakra is the knowledge of the living process. Whereas the knowledge of the dead diverts our attention to the collective subconscious area by which we become prone to outside interference of the collective dead. All the nightmares of Pandora's Box are unleashed when we allow these influences to dominate us. No matter how helpful or informative, any attempt to communicate with the dead is an invasion of our own being. Our inspiration comes from our own direct connection with the all-pervading power of Divine love when our kundalini is sustained in the central channel. There is no need for any other medium.

More recently, Dr Z.V. Harvalik, an engineer working for a US Army agency and vice president of the American Society of Dowsers, claims to have identified the receptors in the body by which dowsers receive and process their sense impressions. After a series of laboratory tests using various forms of metal shielding to block off parts of the body in turn, he located the suprarenal glands (over each kidney) as a major receptor area.

When the body receptors do not run according to the frequency of the chakras, they get entangled in alien channels. These unfriendly channels are the dead entities or units of psychic interference (UPI) that hover in the collective subconscious or the collective supraconscious because they are stagnant or unable to evolve. Their behaviour pattern is similar to parasites that desperately latch on to another entity for survival. In the normal course, they cannot penetrate a spiritually strong individual. However, sometimes when an individual's attention is lost, his mind wavers into the frequency of a UPI, and at that moment, the mind is susceptible to the UPI. If the individual is weak, then it is easy for the UPI to secure its hold. Gradually, the UPI superimposes upon the individual and enslaves it.

At the physical level, the second chakra governs the functions of the kidneys, liver, pancreas, spleen and intestines. It breaks down fat particles in the abdomen to replace the grey and white cells in the brain. Thus, it regenerates the faculty of thinking, planning, creativity and aesthetics. The liver is a vital organ and generates the energy for brain activity and also removes toxins from the blood.

Attention is another energy generated by the liver. In the Purshottam Yog of the Bhagvad Gita, according to Lord Krishna, our roots grow in the brain, and its branches (attention) spread downwards. As the attention moves downwards to the Mooladhara Chakra, it is attracted by sex. But if the attention gets obsessed with sex, it becomes susceptible to domination and thus, gets entangled in sexual perversions.

Furthermore, the presence of alcohol in the liver changes the structure of the water in it, and it no longer cools the liver. This is the reason most alcoholics suffer from liver problems. An irate liver fritters away the attention, which reflects restlessness and an angry temperament. A seeker with a weak or a hot liver finds it hard to meditate because his scattered attention does not allow thoughtless awareness to settle. A stable attention span is a prerequisite for meditation.

Artificial behaviour dulls the sensitivity of the second chakra. Artificial behaviour takes us away from the beauty, aesthetics and peacefulness of life. By reducing the abstract to crude artificial behaviour, the vision of reality is eclipsed. Those who try to be someone they're not often end up depressed. Depression is the polarity of the impressions we try to cast on others. Sweet fragrance does not come from plastic flowers. If one interacts with people through a projection, then how can one drink their sweet nectar? At most, one can become a social butterfly who will likewise only attract the digital. The other polarity of casting impressions is jealousy. In this competitive world, when one person succeeds, those left behind feel jealous and try to pull him down. The ego generates a sense of jealousy because it gets hurt.

Shakespeare aptly said, 'To thine own self be true'. When we are true to ourselves, we speak from the heart. The truest expression of ourselves reflects radiantly on our face and behaviour, and thus, touches another person's heart. On the other hand, the ambition to claim superiority over others or be widely acclaimed for one's intellectual acumen sources from the ego. Spontaneity is absent from all ambitious and competitive efforts, and this explains why conceptual art lacks the vitality of the living process.

Both individual and the collective conditioning reflect in the works of an artist. However talented or passionate an artist may be, the ambit of their creativity is limited to their conditioning or intellect—for instance, a poet who laments over broken love affairs projects from the subconscious. Creativity that does not touch another's heart is like a flower without any fragrance or like hippy culture that left its soul behind!

On the other hand, the kundalini opens the door of intuitive creativity that would otherwise take an artist a lifetime to unlock. Thomas Edison pointed out, 'If we did all the things we are capable of doing, we would literally astound ourselves.' Indeed, we are not aware of our intuitive creativity. Intuitive creativity is not borrowed, superimposed or pirated—it is original. Intuitive creativity is felt unconsciously and manifests auspiciousness. Auspiciousness is the co-efficient of beauty and exudes vibrations. The music maestro A.R. Rahman said something similar, 'What I get from spirituality, I give to music.'

The gaze of a realized artist pierces the human heart and experiences the warmth and coldness of each person with whom they come into contact. Through the pain of humanity collected in their own heart, the artist breathes the vibrations of their kundalini into the hearts of others and, in turn, wires others to their kundalini. The vibrations of their kundalini start flowing and liberate the pain collected in their heart. Thus, a realized artist resurrects as a messiah, a prophet. As William Blake said, 'Men of God shall become prophets, and have the power to make other prophets'.

8

CHAKRA OF DHARMA AND PROSPERITY

I hope everybody could get rich and famous and will have everything they ever dreamed of, so they will know that its not the answer.

—Jim Carrey

The population of this world has been increasing steadily, and different groups and nations have been trying to get their share of the limited resources. This is compounded by the growing aspirations of individuals, groups, states, countries, being influenced by technology, mass media, etc. The direct result is an increased state of competition between individuals, groups, countries at all conceivable levels. But the show must go on—we must continue to do our work and meet deadlines over prolonged durations.

As the show goes on, the postmodern audience is mesmerized by the suspense and intrigue of the drama of modern life and, in the bargain, loses sight of its innate living process. Any attempt to reconnect with the living process through rationality proves futile because our rationality is not mature enough yet. Nonetheless, it is possible to reconnect

Nabhi Chakra

through our indwelling power of the kundalini. To draw attention into her realm, one has to be subtle. Shri Mataji Nirmala Devi reveals how to witness the show with the eyes of the kundalini:

> Carbon has four valences. Gold has the property that it cannot be tarnished. Similarly, human beings have ten valencies. These are within us to give us balance. In the case of chemical combinations, if one valency is missing, it becomes negative and then combines with another. So there are negative and positive valencies. Man has evolved from an amoeba to this stage, through these ten valencies, which is the code of law of evolution or dharma. This code of life protects and nourishes our spiritual growth.

Human evolution, on the third step, was sustained by dharma. The third step of evolution also evolved the third chakra, or the solar plexus, that sustains human ascent. The sustaining force helped us to harness nature's resources and become prosperous. Prosperity coined the American dream, and success became synonymous with the number of zeros on one's check. It led to the the false belief that the more money you have, the more others will love you. So began the lust for money. But, when the curve of prosperity dipped into recession, the American dream turned into a nightmare. However, it was not just the recession; it was something deeper in the American psyche that had made them compulsive buyers—it was the restlessness of their seeking.

In 2011, students at the University of Washington asked Bill Gates how he felt about being a billionaire. He laughed, 'Once you get beyond a million dollars, it's the same hamburger.

I'm certainly well taken care of in terms of food and clothes. Money has no utility for me beyond a certain point. Its utility is entirely in building an organization and getting the resources out to the poorest in the world.'

Then in 2013, he said to *The Telegraph*, 'I have no use for money. This is God's work.'

Money is a great way to satisfy our material desires, but instead, if it leads to stress, there is a problem! In the Bhagvad Gita, Lord Krishna advises Prince Arjuna to earn a lot of money only so that it could be given to the needy. It finds resonance in the persona of the Goddess of wealth, Lakshmi. She receives with one hand and gives with the other. After all, if a poor man needs money and nobody has it to give him, how will he be helped? Sahaja Yoga experiments have revealed that this chakra bestows eight blessings—prosperity, auspiciousness, dignity, spiritual ascent, pure knowledge, domestic and collective joy, wealth and success. Thus an auspicious third chakra empowers us to do more with less.

However, we may think we have it all, but no one has it all without losing something in the bargain. By having a lot more of something, we have too little of others. Despite all the wealth, the 'haves' are as much stressed as the 'have-nots'. Nor does peace come from success; often, people take to drinking and self-indulgence to beat stress. However, there is a great way to overcome stress—through kundalini awakening. As the kundalini empowers the third chakra, it remaps every aspect of daily life—health, economy, art, culture and politics. According to the Russian artist Nicholas Roerich, 'Where there is culture, there is peace, there is achievement, there is the right solution for any given problem.'

Indeed the problems of poverty, population and economy

can be solved through strengthening the third chakra, and that's how the nabhi chakra of the world can transform.

At the physical level, the right-side petals of the chakra nurture our liver. The liver is like a steam engine that kicks off our financial health, business drive, futuristic planning and logic. In cases of hectic lifestyles, futuristic thinking or financial worries, the overworked engine catches fire and spreads to the spleen. In ancient Greece and medieval humoral medicine, few organs were more crucial than the spleen. It was associated with laughter and happiness, and poems were written about it. Nineteenth-century women with depression were said to be plagued by illnesses of the spleen. Emergency signals received by the spleen make it function in a frantic manner. The spleen is the speedometer of the body, and thus, the emergency buttons that we press could be driving the spleen crazy, and likewise, could also make other people hectic.

The nabhi chakra also looks after digestion. There are thousands of neurons in the stomach. Hence, it is a very sensitive receptor. Can you imagine how much electricity is needed for a liquidizer? The stomach performs a much greater function despite all the ill-treatment it receives. In contrast, a liquidizer would break down if a small pin was missing in its machinery. Eating habits excite the glands that secrete digestive enzymes—if one is hurried, angry or worried, the food is not digested properly because the stomach muscles become tense and impair their secretion. Not just that—people who cannot relax do not allow others to relax. Whereas, with a relaxed nabhi chakra, we enjoy watching how things spontaneously come our way.

However, too much attention to food creates a mental appetite, where we eat more than our body needs. The stomach's hunger can be satisfied by food, but not the hunger of the mind. Why worry about food as long as it is wholesome and nourishing? Two thousand years ago, Hippocrates said, 'Let food be thy medicine.'

Nor is fasting the answer! Nobody attains God through fasting. It is a myth that the body is purified by fasting. Purification does not come from fasting or penance but from a change of heart. Kabir said, 'What will you gain by turning the beads of the rosary if you have not turned within?'

The stomach needs a regular routine and a proper diet. Fasting may be resorted to under special circumstances of health, but other than that, it has no spiritual significance. What use is fasting if the mind keeps thinking of food? The Upanishads say, 'The whole world is the garment of the Lord. Renounce it, and, then receive it back as the gift of God.'

The image of a seeker as an ascetic runs deep in ritualistic cultures. But the one who desires worldly pleasures and the one who desires to renounce them are both on the same footing, for they both nurture desire. Only the cool vibrations of the kundalini can put out the fire of desire in the nabhi chakra. As the seeker does not get attached to anything, he does not have to give up anything. Thereafter, the kundalini awakens the chakra's innate quality of patience—patience with others and oneself. But as Jonathan Morrs said, 'Patience is a virtue; possess it if you can. Seldom found in woman, never found in man.'

We get frustrated when we see our life scripted out, but we are not robots—nature takes its own course. We have to wait for the maturing process patiently. Among all the elements of the nabhi chakra, patience is supreme. After all, this gift of the nabhi chakra allows us to sit back and relax while others argue, not feeling the need to convince or control. Although a patient person cares, he can just relax while everyone else worries about the next snowstorm, economic downturn or even the end of the world, for that matter.

However, patience should not be mistaken for fatalism because there is no passive resignation to fate here. On the contrary, there is a conscious attempt to cool down the anxiety pouring down from the other chakras. In the Bhagavad Gita, Lord Krishna advises us to do our allotted duty well and not worry about the reward. Hence, a great way to stop worrying is by knowing that we made the right effort.

Domestic peace is an essential attribute for drawing the restlessness in the nabhi chakra to a peaceful mode. Domestic instability constricts the left-side petals of the chakra. If the wife is not respected, this chakra gets constricted. Conversely, a stable chakra engenders peace and propels healthy relationships. It not only brings forth peace within, but also has the power to bring peace to others.

9

THE OCEAN OF ILLUSION

*But even Satan cannot enter you
until he has found a flaw.*

—Yogi Mahajan

Since the dawn of human evolution, there has been a constant battle against ignorance and illusion. The state of ignorance has to be overcome before seekers can experience the reality of their living process. As human beings prospered and their basic needs were satiated, their inner quest sought this reality. Through their limited intellect, they could not connect with the living process, and hence, they prayed for guidance. When we want to go to another city, we seek someone who has been there before for the directions. Likewise, on our inward journey, we do not walk the road alone; the Primordial Masters walk with us—Lao Tzu, Dattatreya, Raja Janak, Sai Nath of Shirdi (late nineteenth century), Socrates, Abraham, Moses, Confucius, Zoroaster, Prophet Mohammed and Guru Nanak paved the stepping stones. Admittedly, their teachings have become distorted, and opportunists have turned their dream into a nightmare of power and pecuniary adventurism.

The area that represents the struggle to cross over from

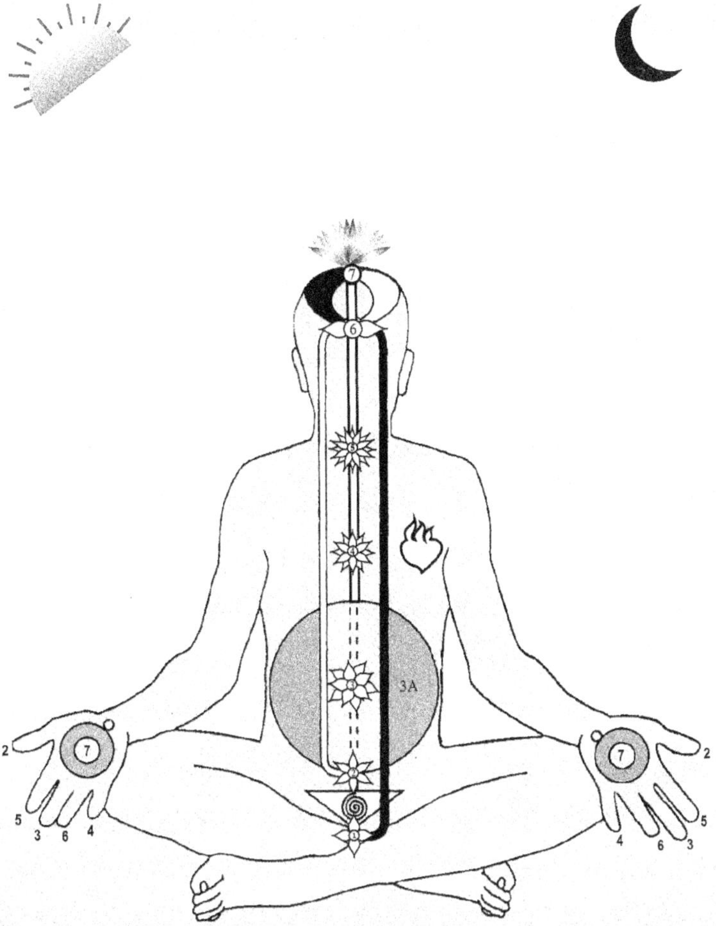

Void

illusion to reality is known as the void or Bhavasagara (Ocean of illusion). It revolves around the second and the third chakra, to filter out all the aspects of ignorance and illusions collected in the chakras. In a sense, it represents the vacuum that separates our conscious mind from reality. Once we know the Absolute, we can know the relative. Till then, a grey area comes in the way of the void that confuses us between negativity and positivity. To cross the sea of illusion, we have to wake up to the difference between the negative and the positive, and realize that there is nothing in between. The molecules and atoms have vibrations, and there is no matter without vibrations—all falsehood that we accept stops the vibrations.

Opportunities attract opportunists; the glitter of gold attracts thieves, and the seeking in the void attracts fake gurus. A naïve seeker is oblivious of their game plan and easily gets hooked by those who pamper his ego. As the fake guru speaks in the name of God, the seeker is deceived into accepting him as his spiritual master and readily becomes his slave.

We like to believe that we alone are capable of controlling our choices and decisions. But what if they are not fully under our control, but under the possession of a false guru or a cult? More particularly, we are liable to fall under the influence of a domineering personality. Having submitted our free will, we voluntarily accept the authority of the cult leader or a religious fanatic. False gurus are good at exploiting our weaknesses by blocking our void with their egos. We get caught up with their cosmetic personality, charisma and mind talks. How can we evolve under the heavy load of falsehood if we chain ourselves to them through our own free will? Christ talked of possessions and cleansed people by throwing out the evil spirits as well. He cast forth demons from madmen by the Sea of Galilee.

In other words, he re-established the control of the victim's conscious mind over the superimposing will of a dead spirit.

The dead spirit possesses because they are like parasites who nurture their desires by feeding on the human mind. For instance, an alcoholic spirit desires alcohol, but as he cannot get it, he possesses a human being who is alcoholic. He captivates the victim's mind in a weak moment and urges him to drink more. Thus, he satiates his own urge through the victim's mind experience. In this way, dead spirits, psychic forces or UPI use human beings.

The research of American neuropsychiatrist Dr Elmer Green of the Menninger Foundation, Kansas, who has worked over 15 years as a physicist on rockets and guided-missile research, is profound:

> According to various warnings, the persistent explorer in these realms...brings himself to the attention of indigenous beings who, under normal circumstances, pay little attention to humans... Systems for inner exploration describe these indigenous beings as entities whose bodies are composed entirely of emotional, mental and ethereal substance, and say that at this level of development they are psychologically no better than an average man himself. They are of many natures and some are malicious, cruel and cunning, and use the emergence of the explorer out of his previously protective cocoon with its built-in barriers of mental and emotional substance as an opportunity to move, in reverse so to speak, into the personal subjective realms of the investigator. If he is not relatively free from personality dress, it is said; they can obsess him with various compulsions for their

> own amusement and in extreme cases can even disrupt the normally automatic functioning of the nervous system, by controlling the brain through the chakras. Many mental patients have made the claim of being controlled by the subjective entities, but the doctors in general regard these statements as part of the behavioural aberration, pure subconscious projections, and do not investigate further.

Interesting, too, is his suggestion that they may influence the brain through the chakras. The notion that indigenous entities act on them parallels the traditional Christian teaching that the evil spirit takes his stand at the gateway between sense and the Spirit, making its impact, not at the deepest point of the Spirit, but upon the imagination.

This is how people go into a trance or conduct seances. People who claim to be psychic or clairvoyant and possess supernatural powers are unaware of how they have this faculty, nor can they pass it on to others. This is because it is not their own faculty but the power of the UPI possessing them. The human faculties of an average individual are not shrouded in any mystery. Everyone is aware of them, and they can be easily explained. Such possession by a UPI is extremely dangerous as it disrupts the harmonious functioning of the sympathetic and parasympathetic nervous systems. By drawing on the energy of the chakras, it exhausts their energy supply. Further, by superimposing itself upon the mind, it interferes with the brain and causes mental disorders. In fact, all body functions are carried on by the autonomous nervous system, over which we have no conscious control, but it is susceptible to outside influences.

This left-side sympathetic nervous system (libido) has the power to store all that is dead in us. It connects us with storehouses of the subconscious mind and also with the collective subconscious (Bhootlok or Parlok). At the back of the brain, at the apex of this channel, sits the superego, much like a balloon. It becomes heavy by storing the conditioning of the mind through the libido. If the tension is heavy, it breaks the superego into many fragments. If one still overexerts by conditioning, a partial vacuum is created, which sucks another dead personality from the collective subconscious (Parlok) into one's superego. Hence, in the pursuit of truth, if one takes to further efforts, and indulges in the deliberations of the mind such as forced abstinence, forced meditation or complete slavery to emotional attachment, the libido, with the aid of the affected superego, may connect to the collective subconscious where all dead souls—bad, good or saintly—exist. These souls start manifesting through one's personality, and one gets siddhis or extrasensory perceptions. Actually, these are the different subtle (dead) personalities dominating the personality through the superego.

There is another method that many so-called teachers may effortlessly employ, by which they turn the chakra in the direction of the libido, which can result in one slipping into the subconscious. This method either makes the aspirant go into a trance or leads to them accepting the complete domination of the dead spirits introduced by the teacher through the plexuses.

In the first case, the seeker feels relaxed, and their mind is switched off. After a few years of practice, they realize their weakness—that they cannot face reality. This leads to them resorting to drugs. In the second case, the aspirant becomes a complete slave of the teacher and starts giving away all the material possessions to the teacher without any logic. These teachers never explain the technique that they employ nor do they give their powers to others. All efforts made in the name of so-called religion or mishandling of the kundalini can only activate the sympathetic nervous system, but it cannot make any progress on the sushumna nadi.

All mesmeric powers such as materialization powers (enslaving masses for money, power or fame), visionary powers (Drishti Siddha), speech powers (Vani Siddha), curing powers, transcendental feeling (the power of switching off the mind), separation of body astral travel and many others, are very ordinarily found among those who practice the control of spirits (Pret Siddhi or Samashan Vidya). All such powers can be proven as powers of the dead in any one of the Sahaja Yoga Experimental Centres.

These are not Divine powers because the Divine has no interest in such gross subjects. He is only interested in the miracle of the inner being and its manifestation for human evolution. Those who indulge and use their attention (i.e. chitta) or such powers (siddhi) and those who run after such gross miracles become vulnerable to possession.

Psychic powers do not imply authentic transpersonal mastery. The one who displays them has obviously not transcended ego identifications. In reality, his followers seek the secret of this power rather than their inner self. Such seekers may be misguided—their intent could be self-indulgence, curiosity, selfishness, ambition, or simply greed.

Charlatans have taken advantage of the vacuum created by the decline of traditional and spiritual values. A guru who exercises control over a group through fear or a guilt complex is obviously to be suspected. On the other hand, a guru who pampers their egos is more dangerous. Pride is as much an obstacle to seeking as guilt. A group that wears the colour of its leader also reflects his psyche. A clever guru can also deceive the intellect by his misinterpretation of scriptures. Thus, negativity can also step in through the devil quoting scriptures. A genuine teacher constantly reminds the seeker to attain self-mastery. He tries to free the disciple from himself and aspires to make him his own guru.

The seeker can examine some aspects of the teacher before taking a leap in the dark. At the outset, there should be an inquiry about whether the teacher is all talk. One should question: What attracts me to him? Is it his charisma, sex appeal, eloquence or success? Does he represent a parental figure or a spouse substitute? Is my desire to belong to a group a cover for my own insecurity? Is it escapism or a fad? What is my intent? Do I want power or do I want the truth?

To find the truth, the seeker has to be honest to themselves, and that power of truth safeguards his innocence. However, good intentions do not preclude gullibility unless common sense and intelligence are also used. Many seekers today are led astray by false gurus and have fallen to the extent that they cannot give up these gurus who make them abnormally slavish and blind.

Is it pertinent to question what one has really achieved in such an event? What are the powers of the disciples manifesting? It has been observed that when possessed people confront Sahaja Yoga, they start trembling and shaking like lunatics. Suppose, with great difficulty, such a person reaches the state of self-realization; in that case, they completely lose interest in such powers or their exhibition as they are freed of all extra dead personalities who dominated them. There is no need to pass through the subconscious strata to reach the unconscious. The subconscious is an end in and of itself, and one who enters its realms gets lost. The only direct way is through the sushumna, which is the central path of Ascent.

It is dangerous to dabble in parapsychology or use the powers of the subconscious because they can become uncontrolled and torture the practitioner. Those who are temporarily benefited may later suffer irreparable loss to the body, mind or grace.

Hallucinations and fantasies occur due to external interference in the void. The block at the void forms a curtain of illusion veiling reality. Unless the void is cleared through the grace of an enlightened master, the seeker will drown in the sea of illusion. The void is the embodiment of our guru principle. When it is awakened, we become the guru and can awaken the kundalini of others.

The seekers who have not been blinded by any false guru easily reach the state of realization. The void is kept pure by people who follow a life of human sustenance (dharma). After one's realization is sustained, the dharma is awakened, and then there is no need to know about dos and don'ts. Gradually, all bad habits vanish spontaneously.

New Age icons could also be catalysts of mass hallucination. Though our brains may have become digital, we have not overcome the primitive herd instinct of our subconscious. At the collective level, the instinct to follow others is a mass instinct. Through this mass feeling, competition sets in. Music mavericks manoeuvre this subconscious instinct to excite their fans. Once the fans are excited, they are induced into mass hysteria.

But there could be further sinister ramifications if the fans lose control of themselves. For instance, when mass hysteria is encouraged or allowed to go on unabated, it can turn into mass violence. At the Woodstock '99 music festival, some youngsters set fire to an overturned car. Inspired by the fire, youngsters used cigarette lighters to start bonfires around the stage with tables, tent fabric, boxes—anything they could burn. All Hell broke loose as a mass of youngsters went on a rampage, toppled light stands, speaker towers, smashed beer bottles, and soon, the whole place went up in flames.

Although the individual should endeavour to become collectively conscious, following the herd blindly is not the way consciousness is achieved.

However, altered states of consciousness, illusions or hallucinations should not be mistaken for collective consciousness. Drugs like marijuana throw us into the subconscious, which may temporarily relieve tensions. Likewise, drugs like LSD throw us into the supraconscious where we conjure our wildest dreams. In both cases, we move away from our axis, and as we lose control of ourselves, we become vulnerable to negative energy which penetrates through a porous subconscious. However, with the aid of our kundalini's vibrations, it is possible to get rid of this. As we return to our axis, the periphery loses its impact on us. Thus, we attain self-mastery and can check out everything with vibrations; if the vibrations are conducive—we go for it, else we let go.

> We know no thoughts of vengeance
> Within this temple's walls
> Where love calls back to duty,
> Who e'er from duty falls,
> By friendship's kindly hand held fast,

He finds the land of light at last.
Here each to every other,
By mutual love is bound,
And where every sin is pardoned,
No traitor can be found.
Those that this bond cannot unite,
Are unworthy of the light.

—Wolfgang Amadeus Mozart, *The Magic Flute*, 'In Diesen Heil'gen Hallen (Within These Hallowed Halls)'

10

THE MIRACLE WITHIN
(THE HEART CENTRE)

No rules of grammar does it keep
Breaking all barriers the heart leaps
When it opens, the world smiles
Atoms dance, what withers revives
Stagnate pools leave their place
Living waters spring forth with grace
Boulders and Barriers begin to break
Shafts of silence dawn a new wake
All eyes brim full, feelings take shape
Not sad, not happy—what moment this is
When neither tear or sweat leave a trace
Nor salt or spice give it taste
The flavor I savor is not of tongue
This minty mist can't go unsung
Like a dewdrop reveling on a young tulip
Like a sip taken from a honeysuckle tip
Gather these delights in a vessel tall
Still it's not enough to describe it all
The heart song and this silence sweet
Surely this is how Divine breathe greets

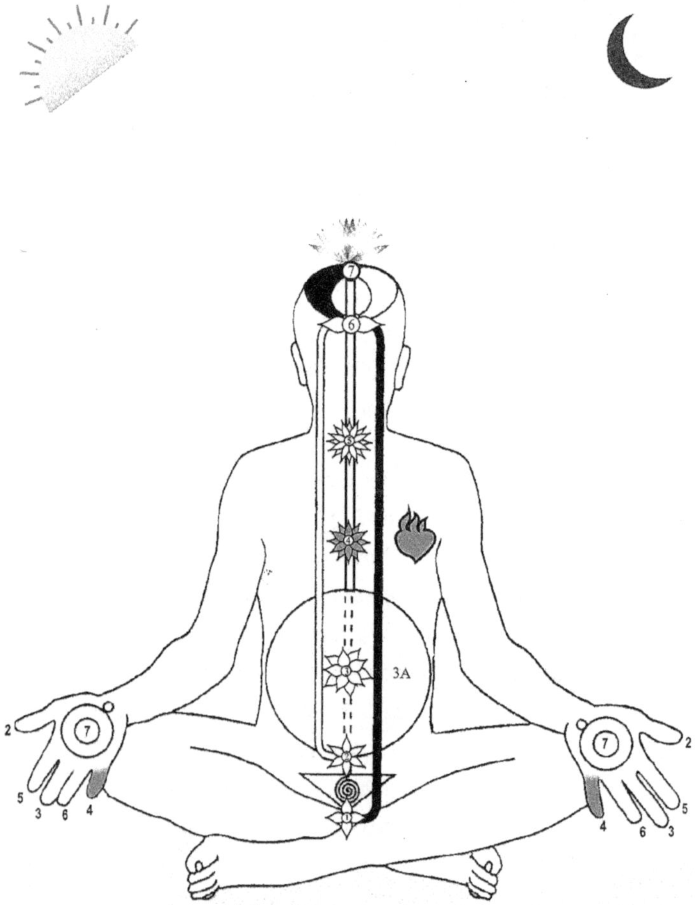

Anahat Chakra

Words attempt but fail to keep
The promise of miracles beyond belief
Words attempt but fail to keep
So I let this melody flow and seep
Forever laying thoughts to sleep.

—Pragya Pradhan

When a child is born, the first thing that they respond to is the spirit of their mother. They are not aware of their identity or that of their mother's, but they feel secure in the warmth of her love. The moment they come out of the mother's womb, they suffer a shock. Their first reaction is to go back into the womb. However, their spirit finds comfort in the spirit of their mother, and through that reassurance, they feel secure in the alien environment. At this stage, their mind, conditioning and ego are not developed. They are cared for by the unconditional love of the spirit.

According to Lord Krishna, the spirit (Atman) resides in the heart chakra,

> The spirit cannot be cut by weapons, fire cannot burn it, water cannot wet it, nor can the wind dry it. Because it is eternal, unchanging, perennial, all-pervading and immovable like a tree. It is unmanifest, unchanging and beyond the intellect. Thus perceive its true nature and do not grieve.
>
> —Bhagavad Gita 2.23–25

It evinces that the Spirit cannot be tainted and nothing can be superimposed upon it. Though the spirit resides in our heart chakra, it is not in our conscious mind. We often mistake temporary happiness for the Spirit. Shri Adi Shankracharya adopts an analytical process of progressively negating all names and forms in order to arrive at its true nature, 'The spirit is neither the mind, intelligence, ego, attention, prana, the elements, the organs, senses nor pleasure and pain, vice and virtue—it is a combination of Pure Consciousness and eternal bliss.'

Shri Mataji Nirmala Devi said, 'Spirit is the collective being within us. We get connected to this collective being within us through our kundalini, and start feeling collective consciousness.'

The Spirit is forever giving—she cannot receive. She is insurmountable. Who can surmount her? She is the empress, content in herself. Though she is sensitive to injustice and wrongdoings, her compassion is so much that she keeps on forgiving but does not compromise her freedom. It has nothing to do with our likes or dislikes—she just loves. Her love is the source of all the joy in the world.

Through her unique discovery of Sahaja Yoga, it is possible to soak our conscious mind in her unconditional love. The more we open our heart, the more the light of the Spirit flows in and drenches our attention with her love. Her love should not be mistaken for an abstract notion or a mental idea; it is as tangible as our heart that beats, for it is none other than love that causes the heart to beat. Too often, love is mistaken for physical attraction. Physical attraction may arise from sex appeal, a dream image of a prince charming, talent, intellectual admiration, or simply a rack appeal. As physical attraction stems from the mind, it cannot be the unconditional love of the spirit because the chemistry of the mind is such that it cannot love; it can only attract. Thus, unconditional love is confused with possessiveness, sex, selfishness and the object of love becomes an object of attachment. Whereas unconditional love is detached; it is behind all creation.

When we talk of love, we should watch the direction of its flow. The new remains so only for a day. For instance, a child gets attached to a new toy, but no sooner does the novelty wear off and the excitement dies. The same is true of relationships based on physical attraction—how else do people who love each other suddenly turn to hate. The attraction could arise from conditioning, a superimposition of an impression or even a wilful deception. Seductive arts are often used to ensnare a good catch. Shakespeare aptly describes it as the fancy of the eyes in his play, *The Merchant of Venice*:

> Tell me where is fancy bred,
> Or in the heart or in the head?
> How begot, how nourished?
> Reply, reply.
> It is engender'd in the eyes,
> With gazing fed, and fancy dies
> In the cradle where it lies.

It is easy to impress people with the outside veneer, but when the eyes become pure, no 'fancy [is] bred'—no greed or lust breeds in the eyes. There is no reaction to an attractive person, but one develops a rapport of oneness with that person.

Of course, there is no need to put up a show, but everything appears yellow to a jaundiced eye. As our attention goes to the faults of others, we absorb their negative vibrations. But the kundalini detoxifies our eyes of disease and allows us to transform our relationship by empowering their chakras with vibrations. The power of positive vibrations is far greater than any disease. It is possible to get rid of all disease in the world through positive vibrations, provided the person is receptive. As the kundalini comes to our attention, we nurture the chakras of others without reacting and thereby overcome their faults by loving them.

The recognition of the Spirit as the nurturing force is imbued in the customs of many traditional cultures. Their customs honour the Spirit and respect its protocol. For instance, in an Indian custom, as the groom approaches the bride's threshold, she observes the protocol of welcoming his spirit with reverence. Marriage is considered the union of two spirits. In the absence of this recognition, marriage is no better than a casual relationship between two individuals. The insecurity problem in digital cultures does not stem from the lack of money but from the absence of recognition. Casual relationships dry up the heart chakra.

Being in love does not bring the rest of life to a standstill. Just as a man is a son, a brother, a friend, a father, a woman is also a daughter, a sister, a friend, a mother and a person with her own pursuits. It does not imply that one's spouse is not the most important focus, but that each one allows the other some space. If the heart is in its right place, then both are equal partners, like the two wheels of a cart. But wrinkles start appearing when one partner dominates the other or is possessive. Because of his physical superiority, the man usually fends for the house and becomes the wage earner. Money gives him power that makes him feel superior. In situations where the female is unable to assert her right, she is frustrated, and the anger gets locked in the heart chakra. The absence of love creates a vacuum in the heart chakra, and that's how perversion punches black holes in its petals. The black holes suck the negative energy of fear. As we give fear the power to become fearful, the heart becomes afraid of breaking. Though emotional trauma may close the heart chakra, the kundalini opens it again, and her love keeps us young again!

However, joy does not flow principally from relationships but from the Spirit. The Eternal Truth is that the Spirit without the body can never be happy, whether in an individual or in a whole people. At the fourth step of evolution, Lord Rama moved the needle to help us change the way we look at things. His exemplary life revealed that unconditional love is like the sap of a tree that flows to all the branches—children, parents, brothers, sisters, friends, the elderly, society and work. If it only flowed to one branch, the tree would die. As each plant yields seeds to help more plants to grow, similarly, the nature of the spirit is to share. As people share and care, the sap of collective love empowers society. As a king, Lord Rama ruled himself and others through the heart and not the brain. The heart gives inspiration and the brain acts on it. The discretion of the heart guided his policies; the sense of respect flows from the discretion of the heart, be it respect between parents and children, husband and wife, brother and sister, or the individual and the collective.

During Lord Rama's reign, wisdom was synonymous with age—where elders were looked up to for guidance. It helped in the integration and preservation of the family. If the family breaks, society disintegrates. A society may offer social security, but a 'use and throw' culture caps the elderly like medicine bottles whose date has expired. Forgotten people, lost and lonely—this aging population would feel insecure, anyway. Old age is a kind of childhood where not money but love and care hold the keys.

But insecurities can also generate in childhood. If the parents are not kind to children or if a child loses his parents, he can become a volcanic personality. Aggression stems from insecurity. Often childhood traumas punch black holes in our organs. However, the traumas stored in our organs can be unlocked by love. Where a mother's love has been denied in childhood, a fulfilling relationship can help bridge the gap. Love generates self-confidence and armed with it, one develops a relaxed and playful personality that can match the challenges of life like a warrior. In contrast, the darkness of fear cripples our natural immunities, and thus renders us vulnerable to allergies. Psychologists attribute insecurity to be the cause of low self-esteem, but that is not the complete truth—insecurity stems from the ego.

After all, we attract to ourselves what we give out! If we are blocked at the heart chakra, we attract the corresponding mate, perpetuating the problem! Hence, if the heart chakra is in its right place before seeking a relationship, we will share our heart with someone who knows how to love. When we respond from the heart, we overlook the shortcomings of others. For instance, it is not burdensome for a mother to sacrifice for her children—it is a love call. Love is the life-giving force of the family; it bonds, nourishes and sustains it.

Turning our inner gratitude into action empowers the heart chakra. Advanced studies show that people who feel most grateful have greater life satisfaction, fewer visits to the doctor and better sleep. The warmth of a doctor also contributes to his healing power. Like the bee is attracted to the honey spontaneously, the vibrations of a loving person heal. It is not a moral compulsion or a mental decision but the spontaneous response of the heart to pain. The poet George Herbert said it all in his poem, 'Gratefulness':

> Thou has given so much to me.
> Give me one more thing; a grateful heart.

According to Shri Mataji,

> Who is the other? Where the limited capacity of the brain becomes unlimited in its capacity to realize God—if you are the sun and sunlight, if you are the moon and the moonlight, then where is the duality? Only when there is separation, there is duality and because of that separation, you feel attachment. A distance between you and yours; that is why you get attached to it... Everything is we; who is the other? When the brain loses its ego identity, the so-called limited brain becomes the unlimited Spirit.

Compelled by the love of the living process, every part seeks its whole, whereas the ego divides. Where individualism takes precedence over the collective, the spirit is left behind, and the outcome is devoid of joy—moreover, excessive focus on individualism results in loneliness. If ambition sways over the motivation of our soul, people are joyless and bored. Production lines and indiscriminate use of technical solutions for economic growth are programmed to make a kill. Schools are reduced to mass production factories for processing kids into production lines—executives, entrepreneurs, salesmen, etc. Harvard Business School may teach a person to be successful, but it does not teach them how to be happy. Yes, they inject an outsmart bug to race and win, but ironically, in the end, there are no winners. Many successful Japanese business people are increasingly dying of heart attacks at a young age. However successful a person may be, if their heart chakra is closed, they are like a flower without fragrance.

What's in the head does not come from the heart—it's an implant. The attention that gets fixed on the mental plane loses its mobility to catch the joy waves of the heart. A prop may be required to mobilize such attention. But if it drifts into the subconscious, the pendulum movement of extreme and opposite behaviour causes a split personality.

Are we to live in a way that fractures our human bonds and connectivity with our planet? Or shall we live in a way that we are more one with the world?

But how can we be one with the world if we are not one with ourselves?

After realization, it is easy to connect with our spirit because it is within us—it is not borrowed. When the kundalini rises, she enlightens our spirit. As the light of the spirit shines, we enjoy her vibrations and allow them to work out the problems in our chakras. Psychologists probe the rational mind from the outside, but if the chakras are out of gear, the problem merely shifts from one chakra to another. Whereas, if we use the vibrations of the Spirit, and not the effort of the rational mind, we will be surprised how the problems get solved spontaneously. Through successive cycles of such amazing experiences, the ego's hold loosens over the heart. As the pathway of the chakras become free of all encumbrances, we not only witness our faults but also get rid of them completely. Not just that, through her power of love, our kundalini cleanses the defects of others and thus restores their self-confidence. Shri Mataji reveals:

The foundation of our value system is shaken; we have ego, but no self-confidence. Self-confidence comes through our virtues, through the manifestation of our spirit. The greatest virtue is love. How can we love when we analyse everything about everyone? We deaden the person completely by this. Like the sun shines everywhere—it does not see the defects, it just gives, thus, there is no need to judge others.

Throughout Shri Mataji's life, there were daily occurrences where she absorbed the pain of others. Her body was so compassionate that it absorbed their sufferings spontaneously. As patients were brought in her presence, their chakras healed while her body absorbed their pain. She modestly smiled, 'Oh, it's nothing, just my body,' and the patient was healed.

But giant multinational companies are not in the business of healing our pain. They are like a moving vehicle that just doesn't stop—like the bus in the movie *Speed*, which would explode if the driver ever took her foot off of the pedal! In fact, even in a perfect situation, accelerating without balancing the speed with brakes just means danger. We're talking business. We're talking corporate. We're talking about what employers and managers are expecting and rewarding their employees for these days—being super pumped and fierce. Those terms are floating about in the corporate world and are pretty much practised in a lot of large companies. Sounds exciting to be excited, right? To be all pumped and then be rewarded? Sure, but something's missing, and most people feel it even though they can't spot it.

Maybe a sci-fi movie could make it easier to understand—one where we see a giant dominating machine or robotic animal wreaking havoc and crushing what comes in its way. Imagine working under a machine, a non-living entity that only cares that it must be fed more and more to grow bigger. In the real world, many corporations become these non-living, non-feeling entities that just want to 'live' forever no matter how many men or women come and go, profit or perish. The name of the corporate game is, 'Please me at any cost.' And the human game says, 'Sure, if it means more money for me'. Unfortunately, in all this play for money, the most vital living force of the human spirit is pretty much left out or crushed. It cries out in the wilderness of non-entities, wondering if anyone knows what it takes to please a genuine being. It turns away, neglected and desolate, leaving the heart chakra empty and unable to feel joy. That works just fine for companies because in the corporate world, it's not about what pleases one's spirit at all, but it's about what pleases one's ambition. So there we have it—acceleration, determination and push-to-the-limit attitude all wrapped up in the garb of excitement and enthusiasm. Is it worth it? Yes, if our only goal is to be a millionaire, but when has that ever guaranteed joy or even health?

If joy is the goal, then our heart chakra can bring joy back in life if we give it precedence over being super-pumped. Business and functional leaders deal with important decisions that affect the collective every day. Often these decisions are a trade-off between expediency and collective interests. As the right heart opens it, a fatherly attitude takes precedence overproduction. The heart of the management shifts towards the benevolence of the workforce. Business schools teach that positive employee policies reflect in the employees' output. The corporate body realizes that the policies that promote industrial relations also promote industrial production. If the corporate body treats its employees better, big deals will come anyway!

Peace, on the right side of the heart chakra, not only brings joy and satisfaction to the entrepreneur but also to his family and society. Thereafter, the collective understanding that the employer and the employee are a family, helps in healthy relationships. Thus, the health of a society does not arise from game-changing ideas but from a change of heart.

Love has a capacity—it can penetrate matter to express its warmth. For instance, a home built with love is an eternal source of joy. Likewise, love can penetrate government policies, industries and public institutions. After all, what is all the planning for if it does not bring joy to the public? What good do top-heavy bureaucratic structures do other than waste national resources? It is indeed surprising that the nations that allocate the largest health budgets are the ones that generate the greatest health hazards. It is not the financial budgets but a change of heart that transforms public health. As government policies back up the collective heart's innate energy of resilience and wisdom, the collective heart creates concentric ripples of love that transform world health. Indeed, the power of love acts where people share and care.

It is love that makes us compassionate and compels us, without thinking, to extend a hand to others. It is not a moral compulsion or a mental decision but a spontaneous act. The heart responds to another's suffering because it is itself the reflection of the other—there is no 'I' or 'you'; there is just a confluence. In that confluence, we experience human bonding, as the poet Kahlil Gibran expressed, 'And let there be no purpose in friendship, save the deepening of the Spirit.'

Physically, there may be differences in colour, shape, form, mindset or ideology but the heart chakra does not have only one petal—it is a lotus with several petals like patience, forgiveness and forbearance. Similarly, the ego, too, has several petals like hate and jealousy. It is surprising how quickly hate becomes such a cementing force among people. Hate is carried by their ego, but the transcendence of ego does not require violence. If we fight the ego, its reaction merely triggers a recurrence of the same. Thus, the answer is not to go on fighting the old but building the new.

Furthermore, the belief that penance is necessary to overcome the ego, while pleasure is evil, closes the left side petals of the heart chakra, the seat of the Spirit. Neither asceticism nor self-torture dissolves the ego. At the physical level, the heart is the pump of the body—hence, any mental or physical excess strains it. The hot vibrations created by overactivity dry out the petals on the right side of the heart chakra, and as the heat spreads to the left side petals, they too dry up, and that results in a heart attack.

Using the body as an instrument of athletic display fatigues the heart chakra. If we pay attention to our sense organs, what do we achieve? The light is inside, but the light has to come to our attention. That is Yoga. It happens only after self-realization. Likewise, the practice of Hatha Yoga is mainly confined to the physical, and the spiritual aspect is left behind. Around the first century BC, the sage Patanjali codified a holistic system called Ashtanga Yoga. It has eight aspects that include postures, breathing exercises, meditation and introspection. The most important is *ishwar pranidhan*, which means the establishment of God within us. The sage Patanjali prescribed the *yoga chitta-vritti-nirodagh* (to achieve union through the ability to stop thoughts). However, unless our kundalini rises to the agnya chakra, how will she absorb the thoughts? Furthermore, how will we know at which chakra our attention is blocked? If it is blocked at the nabhi chakra and we do exercises for the neck, what is the use? It is like taking the wrong medicine. Hence, to achieve *ishwar pranidhan*, the first step is awakening the kundalini.

Hatha Yoga techniques are adapted to found schools of furniture yoga, wherein it is taught that yoga consists of one sitting on a chair and leaning one way or the other. People need a toy to play with, and by treating our bodies like gadgets, we ourselves become gadgets. Another guru teaches yoga specifically meant for couples. Couples need someone to assure them that they are in love. There is a misconception that we can reach God by wearing saffron robes or foregoing clothes altogether. Kabir said, 'If God could be found by going naked, then the beasts of the forest would have found him long ago.'

It takes all sorts of people to make the world. The ones with a dominant sun channel project the mental program of their sun channel, and the ones with a dominant moon channel project the emotional conditioning of their moon channel. However, our programming need not come in the way of keeping our heart chakra open. It's the nature of the heart chakra to love. We do not need a reason to love because love is the innate nature of our kundalini, just as fragrance is the innate nature of a flower. A flower does not choose whom to give its fragrance. It yields to the bees without asking for anything in return. The nectar of love dissolves people.

As the love of our kundalini gives us confidence, we do not feel the need to aggress others. For instance, a world leader like Mahatma Gandhi was so humble and yet so powerful. He succeeded in freeing his country from the shackles of the mightiest power simply through non-violence because his

Spirit gave him that confidence. Likewise, despite the odds, world leaders like Abraham Lincoln, Martin Luther King Jr. and Nelson Mandela were empowered by their Spirit. Love does not hide—it stands and shines.

The greatest mistake is to close one's heart. However painful the hurt may be, however torn the heart chakra may be; there is someone within who always loves us. She is our individual Mother—our kundalini. As Shri Mataji Nirmala Devi says:

> What is there to be afraid of anyone?
> What is there not to trust anyone?
> What is there to be angry with anyone?
> The easiest thing in the world is to give love from the innocence of your heart.
> You don't have to pay for it.

Indeed, love begets love; no power in the world can stop it. Thus, as the heart chakra of the society opens, the world transforms.

11

THE INSTRUMENT OF LOVE

There is no plant without medicinal quality
There is no human being without some virtue,
Because of our unawareness, we don't see it.

—Shri Matji Nirmala Devi

At the fifth step of evolution, the fifth chakra was opened to express the joy of the Spirit. This chakra is made like a flute to express the music of the Spirit. But the flute has to be hollow to allow its flow. Indeed, the strings of our instrument have to be fine-tuned—if they are too loose, they break, and if they are too tight, they do not play. This art can be learnt from our mothers and grandmothers—how they brought us up in childhood with the sweet music of the heart that we abided by their guidance spontaneously. In that sweet learning process, there was nothing to feel hurt about. Though sweet childhood may be left behind, the fifth chakra plays on the sweet melodies of the Spirit. But too often, the melody gets interrupted by the note, 'Oh, I should not have done it. I feel guilty.'

Vishuddhi Chakra

Shri Mataji reveals:

> Because of your guilty nature, you say things that are harsh. To overcome this block, you should use sweet words. Your language should be sweet to everyone; especially men must speak sweetly to their wives. Now, that sweetness will cure that block. Always speak very sweetly, try to find out all the sweet words. The sweet method of addressing is the best way to cure your guilt because if you say anything harsh to anyone, you may say so as a matter of habit or maybe because you feel happy by saying that, but as soon as you say it, you say, 'Oh, God, what did I say!' That is the biggest guilt. One always has to try to find sweet words. See how the birds are chirping; in the same way you have to learn all the sounds of everything by which you make people happy by your sweetness. It is very important. Otherwise, if your left block grows too much, you will develop a way of talking by which your lips will be distorted towards the left side.

What a great power the Vishuddhi Chakra has to comfort others by speaking sweetly! It did not escape the attention of the great Indian maestros—they harnessed this power to compose ragas. 'Ra' is energy, 'ga' is that which penetrates ether to soothe the chakras. The science of ragas evolved from configurations of mantras that harmonized the chakras. However, the indiscriminate chanting of mantras can dull the vibrations of the chakras by causing self-hypnosis. For instance, a lullaby can put a child to sleep by lulling his senses. Mantras are like monotones that dull the senses. By diverting the attention from the stress and strain on the mind, they may lead to a temporary state of relaxation, but they do not connect us to the living process.

Instead of feeling others through the heart, if we compete with them through the intellect, it comes in the way of our Vishuddhi Chakra. The one who competes is the ego, and the one who recedes is also the ego. In case we recede, our guilt can be exploited to dominate us. We play into the hands of those who make us feel guilty. Church Fathers were well versed with this human propensity and used confession to control their parish. Inversely, by trying to live up to images and rise to their expectations, we lose our self-esteem.

Conversely, in order to measure our own worth, we look towards others and compare their car, home, clothes, etc. For sure, it feels great to be ahead of others, but what matters is how much we love them, and not how far we've left them behind. However, in our concern for others, we assume responsibility for their behaviour, and if their behaviour does not rise to the occasion, we feel ashamed. For instance, each time the husband faltered in public, the ambitious wife felt guilty as though it was her fault.

As we play games with others, we think that they, too, play games with us. How can we love others if we suspect them? If, instead of understanding others, we start judging them, we fuel cynicism.

Cynicism is contagious. As journalists vent their cynicism in print media, it fuels a vicious circle; the public thinks that aggression is a better way of communication. However, it is not true. Shri Mataji Nirmala Devi's solution lies elsewhere:

> Let us now try the power of love. The suggestions of critics, cynics or pseudo-intellectuals have not led us

anywhere. They only see one side of things—that only complicates the issue. A mother's heart is needed because it encompasses everyone's interests. A mother forgives easily. She does not measure the faults of the children but tries to uplift them. Her methods are so subtle and gentle that the correction is done without provoking the ego.

The one who carries the guilt is the ego. If there is no ego, there is no one to carry the guilt. There is no advantage in looking back—better to be free of the heavy load than cave under it! According to Shri Mataji Nirmala Devi, a great way of getting past guilt is to correct it:

> First, let them have realization.
> Let them have their light.
> Let them see for themselves what is the problem.
> Let them feel it and correct it.
> Let them judge themselves.
> That's the best way to overcome guilt.

We have to choose between living with the negativity collected inside our chakras that will consume all our positive energy or putting closure on this painful episode by forgiveness. Let us take the analogy of a car with two gears—one acts and the other reacts. Likewise, there are two gears in the mind—the first gear acts and the second gear reacts. The driver's job is simply to switch gears and not react. Let's suppose we place our kundalini in the driver's seat, and go for a long drive. As we peep out of the window, we may observe some unpleasant traffic in our lane, but if we park in a place of calm and clarity, and remain a silent spectator, the traffic of thoughts will move on without drifting into guilt. The opening of the fifth chakra empowers us to do precisely that. Not just that, it also helps us to rectify our mistakes. On the other hand, they may never be corrected if we go back to guilt. On the contrary, we may become self-indulgent and enjoy our guilt.

Moreover, the negative energy of the clogged guilt passes to the other chakras. At the collective level, the negative vibrations of our chakras are absorbed by the chakras of others and that creates a collective block. After all, if our chakras affect others, and their chakras affect us, it is not so difficult to understand how we are influenced by the collective chakras of our family and society. The collective chakras could influence us from the collective subconscious or the collective supraconscious. That is to say, our blocks need not necessarily be our own—they could also be superimposed.

As our chakras are interconnected, the awakened kundalini in one individual can surmount the negativity accumulated in the collective chakras. Sahaja Yoga's experiment with a Himalayan tribe revealed that as the kundalini of one tribesman was awakened, he overcame his negative conditioning of the customary animal sacrifice. As he overcame his conditioning, the whole tribe surmounted their collective negative conditioning. It did not escape their consciousness that the inspiration to overcome their conditioning came from a source bigger than themselves!

At the fifth step of evolution, Lord Krishna empowered us to overcome our collective conditioning through the art of diplomacy. On the battlefield, as described in the Mahabharata, he revealed how one could play their role on the stage of life without succumbing to guilt. According to him, if we are not the doer, then there is no guilt. attached to our actions. If there is no doer, there is no ego, and without the ego, there is no one who carries the guilt. His trick was to attribute all action and mental activity to the Primordial Being, who gives us collective consciousness. In this sense, we start feeling our chakras as well as the chakras of others at our fingertips. It is not a myth or a conception but an actualization in our central nervous system. Like an egg becomes a bird, one is reborn into a dimension one did not know existed.

In the epic battle of Mahabharata, Lord Krishna fuelled the forces of good against evil. Evil thrives when good men do nothing. That is to say that the battle of Mahabharata instigated by Lord Krishna was not for random killing but to recognize that the individual life that we call our own is precious only in so far as we accord the same value to the life of all other beings, including beings who oppose our faith. However, in modern times, dharma is exploited by fundamentalists and terrorists.

At the physical level, many nerves passing through the fifth chakra converge at a sub-plexus located at the point between the eyes and the bridge of the nose called the Hamsa Chakra. The understanding of good and evil comes from the discretion of the Hamsa Chakra. This chakra allows us to remove the chaff from the grain, the eternal from the transitory, the reality from the myth, and, more importantly, to see things as they are. When the chakra opens, we get the wisdom of handling people, the wisdom of handling jobs and the wisdom of handling difficult situations.

Indeed, the whole discretion of the cosmos rests in this chakra, but the innocence of the Mooladhara Chakra fuels the quality of discretion.

Knowledge is of no use without discretion, just as a mirror is of no use without the eyes. As Albert Einstein said, 'Everyone is a genius. But if you judge a fish by its ability to climb a tree, it will live its whole life believing that it is stupid.'

A Sufi mystic used to earn his living by selling all sorts of odds and ends. It seemed that the man had no judgment because people would frequently pay him in bad coins and he would accept them without a word of protest.

When it was time for him to die, he raised his eyes to heaven and said, 'Oh God, I have accepted many bad coins from people, but never once did I judge them in my heart. I just assumed that they were not aware of what they did. I am a bad coin too. Please do not judge me.'

And a voice was heard that said, 'How is it possible to judge someone who does not judge others?'

The fifth chakra is the first filter of the body at the physical level—it is a very sensitive centre and guards against outside viruses. Pollution chokes it. A smoker finds it difficult to quit tobacco not because he is weak-willed but because nicotine subverts his willpower. Thus, because of his unawareness, he does not see it.

However, after self-realization, the kundalini empowers his will to get rid of his addiction. Thus, with this enlightened awareness, the Spirit expresses itself and empowers the individual to correct his fifth chakra spontaneously.

12

THE THRESHOLD

'Must I tear them out?'
The peacock protested;
'These gorgeous plumes which
Only tempt my pride.'
Of all his talents
Let the seeker beware.
Aiming for the bait.
He does not see the snare.
Beware of the ego that
Pampers thy wills and skills.
Else there is no bane
So deadly as free will.

—Yogi Mahajan

During a soccer game, players often kick their opponent on the shin. But that does not stop the game—the victim continues to play and even scores a goal or two. If his attention drifts even for a moment, the opponent takes control of the ball, bringing the whole team down. Similarly, in the game of life, we face people who hurt us intentionally or unintentionally. If our focus stays on the hurt, our thoughts get obsessed with how to get at them. They gain control of

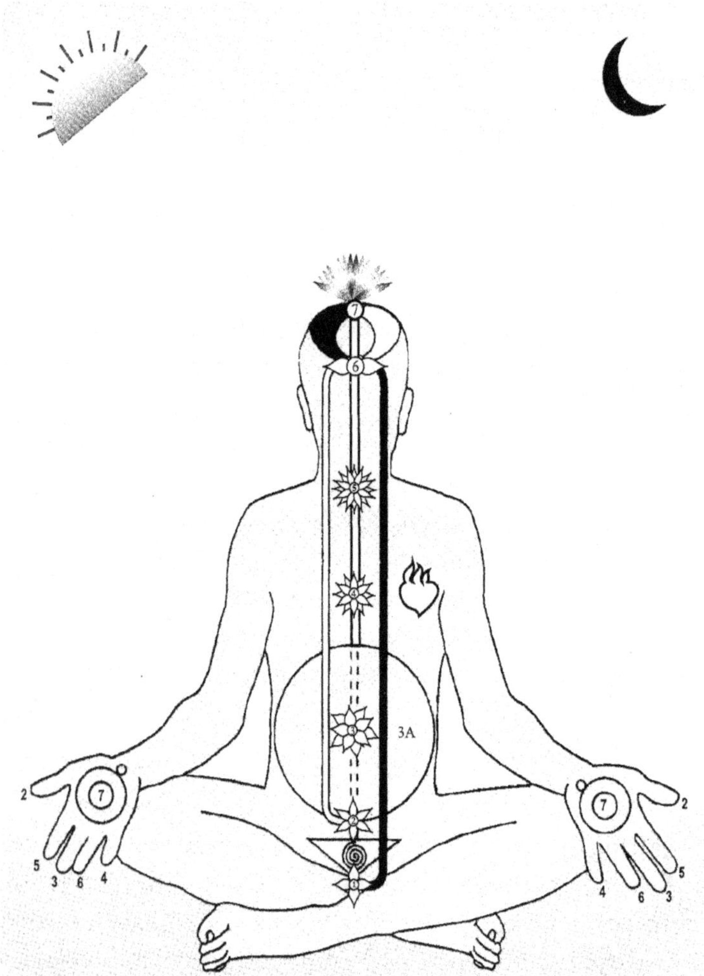

Agnya Chakra

our thoughts in the process, and we lose the game.

The game of life starts in childhood, where parents praise the commonplace acts of their children beyond reason. Their excessive adulation swells the ego. Later in life, others pop or prick the ego. In fact, the ego does not allow us to forgive.

However, the ego does not see itself, but has the capacity to see the ego of others. It is possible to see one's ego if the mind becomes empty like a hollow flute. The flute becomes hollow if it ceases to think it is the doer. And that is only possible if it does not claim credit for its actions. At the sixth step of evolution, three great messengers came to empty our flute: Lord Buddha, Lord Mahavira and Lord Jesus Christ. Lord Buddha pointed to the middle path. Lord Mahavira prescribed the path of non-violence, and Lord Jesus Christ scripted the recipe for forgiveness.

Christ allowed himself to be crucified and forgave those who crucified him. Thus, he enabled us to witness the tyranny of the ego, and thereby unblock the flute. It also unblocked the myth that we have to atone for the sins of our previous lives. This theory was alright before the advent of Christ, but not thereafter. Christ opened the door for our karmas to be absorbed. When the kundalini rises, the door of our sixth chakra—which is nurtured by Christ—opens and allows the kundalini to erase our karmic imprints. Our kundalini's force is great and the whole ego can be dissolved instantly. According to Shri Mataji Nirmala Devi, 'Karmas are accumulated in your ego. When the kundalini rises to the sixth centre, it sucks the ego. When the ego is sucked in, there is no karma.'

Our vengeance against the person who hurts us transfers to an entity that seeks the sympathy of friends—how they have wronged us, how unfair the world treated them etc. The entity seeking revenge is none other than the ego, and as it does not know how to deal with its venom, it fuels sadism: 'If the murderer has escaped, then let his son be hanged.'

Whether we forgive or don't, what can we do to the other? Besides, the person who is not forgiven remains unaffected. Often we hear people say, 'I can never forgive!' It is their ego that does not allow them to forgive. The greater the ego, the greater is the resistance to forgiveness. The important thing is not to fight the ego; if the ego is confronted, it gets fuelled further. The only way to connect with people's hearts is to forgive them and ourselves. The greatest beneficiary is the person who forgives. We don't forgive for the offender's sake; we do it for ourselves. Non-forgiveness fans the ego, whereas forgiveness is a game-changer because the person who is forgiven ceases to sit on our heads! Not just that, when we forgive, we love, and when we love, our spirit's light shines on us.

But wait, when we forgive, it not only releases the negativity from our chakras but also releases the guilt buried in the Vishuddhi Chakra of the offender. Indeed, people's faults can be cured by loving them—what sweeter revenge can there be than forgiveness? When we forgive, the kundalini baptizes us with incredible vibrations.

Shri Mataji reveals, 'Your freedom is in enjoying the freedom of others, not abandonment. After realization, freedom lies in understanding the freedom of others, and not just your own. This is how you will get over your aggressiveness.'

While working on his painting 'The Last Supper', Leonardo da Vinci became very angry with his assistant. Returning to his canvas, he attempted to work on the face of Jesus, but his flute was blocked, and he was unable to resume work. No sooner had he put down his brush and asked forgiveness from his assistant than his flute became hollow, and he finished painting the face of Jesus!

The human brain is wired to forgive people. According to psychologist Molly Crockett of Yale University, 'The brain forms social impressions in a way than can enable forgiveness...the human mind is built to maintain social relationships, even when partners behave badly.'

The teachings of Sahaja Yoga are now being confirmed by psychologists. In the words of William Johnston, Director Institute of Oriental Religions, Sophia University, Tokyo:

> One of the most damaging traumas that can exist in the memory is suppressed anger and refusal to forgive. Because of early wounds, people refuse to accept others (you are not okay) and to accept themselves (I am not okay), and end up in emotional upheaval. Often the root problem is an unconscious refusal to love and to forgive their parents. And this makes it difficult to love and forgive anyone, because we are forever projecting parental images onto the people we meet. One may succeed in forgiving the conscious mind (and this is enough for salvation) but the unconscious lags behind, leaving our love so much less human.

Indeed, Christ is the door, but he is not the destination—the destination is to become the Spirit. He said, 'Behold the Mother'—the Holy Mother reflects within as our Spirit. By Baptism, he meant to awaken this ancient force 'kundalini', which had been sleeping in the human body for generations. The fontanel bone area is the aperture to enter into the all-pervading power of Divine Love (*Brahma Shakti*). The real baptism is its opening (*brahmarandhra*).

The peacock's vanity of its beautiful plumage reminds us that human endeavour, unless aware of the living process, becomes subservient to the ego. As the kundalini opens the door of the sixth chakra—the Agnya Chakra—we enter the realm of the Spirit. Christ has already said that only those who are innocent as children will be allowed to pass through the gates of the Kingdom of God.

However, to enter the kingdom of God, we have to heed the message of the prophets and not reduce them to idols—to follow the spirit of the Buddha, not Buddhism; the essence of Christ, not Christianity. By having a picture of a Rolls Royce around the neck and believing we are riding in a Rolls Royce, will we be able to move even an inch? Fundamentalists get stuck to the letter of the scriptures and miss out on the essence of the prophets. We cannot afford to compromise with darkness or wrong notions about God for our evolution. We should not mind if someone calls it God, the feminine principle or energy; after all, God does not have an address, does he? What matters is the awareness that there is a super-intelligence greater than us, and we are a part of it.

Of course, the intellect has its own limitations and cannot conceptualize it. Conceptual knowledge is like reading a signpost; experience it is like entering it. Moreover, as our attention gets glued to conceptual knowledge, we only see one side of the coin. But life is both. For instance, what we consider 'good' is often a one-sided version of what makes the ego happy. The ego loves to play games and, like children, builds castles in the air only to fnd them broken later. Too often, it gets caught in its own beliefs. Belief is artificial and has no proof behind it. We cannot judge a situation correctly unless we take a balanced view. We cannot trust our emotional response to someone or something unless we can induce ourselves to take an understanding view of the situation. Likewise, the limited prism of the intellect does not always see things as they are; it is influenced, lured, mesmerized, indoctrinated, dominated and deceived by a sharper intellect. Not just that, it deceives itself. If rationality is stretched beyond its limits, it gets corrupted into cunningness. For instance, if we get into the habit of telling lies, we end up lying to ourselves. A cunning landlord made a wager with God, 'If my land sold for a million, I would donate half of it to charity'. After the deal was clinched, the cunning and sharp intellect devised a way to outsmart God. He reworded the deed of sale: 'The price of the land one pound, and the sale of his dog a million.'

For sure, the intellect finds ways to outsmart others, but it creates a polarity that outsmarts it in the bargain. An aggressive sun channel creates a rain-shadow that weakens the moon channel on the other side. When we fall into its trap, our perception of the material world through sense-experience is not reality. For instance, we see a mirage in the desert and mistake it for a water body. The debunking of absolute objective reality strongly resembles Einstein's Theory of Relativity. The only difference is that Einstein provided mathematical muscle to his version of maya (illusion). Those who curate digital images of themselves for the world to see, fall for the maya that if they are great, people will love and respect them, not knowing that it arouses their jealousy. Of course, one cannot always be ahead of others—there is always someone more accomplished, better-skilled, more successful or better looking.

New Yorkers warn visitors not to call anyone on Monday mornings. It is rather surprising because one would imagine that after a long weekend they would be relaxed. On the contrary, the Monday-morning syndrome seems to arise from something else. Firstly, they inch their way through heavy Friday traffic to reach their weekend destination. Next, they busy themselves with pursuing the schedule they fix for themselves. Then, on Sunday afternoon, as they head home, they are held up in the traffic, and thus, reach home irritable and exhausted. Therefore, it is not surprising that they wake up on a Monday morning in a bad mood. Perhaps, they are under the spell of maya, that whispers, 'You have to travel every weekend to find fun.' Not knowing that fun enjoys speed. Speed accelerates excitement. But excitement is not joy. Excitement is born from illusions, whereas joy comes from love. Illusions deceive attention. For instance, the greatest illusion is the fashion industry, where a tag of a certain designer hikes the price of the product! Businesses in Hong Kong and Taiwan are quick to jump on the train. They turn around copies of the designer wear at one-fourth the price!

Too much data, reasoning and analysis make it impossible to escape maya. After Michelangelo finished painting the vault of the Sistine Chapel, the pope found it too plain and instructed him to embellish the colours with gold. Michelangelo responded, 'Holy Father, in those days, men did not wear gold, and those who are painted were not rich.' But the pope was lost in his own maya.

Maya is like quicksilver—just as a person thinks, 'Ah! I have overcome the maya of the ego,' the ego slips into a silent mode like a seemingly egoless person who inadvertently enjoys social recognition. But we can also walk out of maya; for instance, if we are impressed by someone who owns a Ferrari, we should ask, 'Is he going to give it to us?'

As the ego engulfs the whole head and also the heart, the person becomes emotionless. He projects his own ideology, and finds nothing wrong in killing those who oppose it. In fact, in the name of God, suicide bombers think that they attain heaven by killing people they have never met before. It allows us to see more clearly how they are programmed like robots. As their software does not include feelings—their emotional quotient is neglected. Moreover, if the software gets corrupted by a hate virus, then they are capable of committing the most heinous crimes. They are deceived by their own rationale. Thus, the rationale can be used to camouflage untruth as truth. Under the spell of its camouflage, we say, 'Oh, I believed it was so, but later, I realized that I was under a misconception.' Often, our beliefs are based on logical deductions. Logic cuts both ways; we can kill with it or get killed by it. What can be proved by logic can also be disproved by it, as in the case of a clever lawyer who skillfully uses logic to convince the jury to send the innocent to the gallows and let the culprit scot-free. While politicians use rationality to garner votes, salespeople are not far behind to dig into our pockets. They hook customers by offering one shirt free for every shirt they buy. The customer's one-track logic does not tell him that the cost of the free shirt is hidden in the price of the shirt he buys. Marketing czars bleach us in their brainwashing machines. They colour our choices; the model of our car, our holidays, our taste buds and even the kinds of clothes we wear. We can't resist their deception because they know our buttons and press them ruthlessly.

Nor is it possible to detect their deception with our intellect because the intellect is like a blind spot that cannot see itself. The intellect likes to dictate, and hence can be dictated to. It tries to impress and, therefore, can be impressed. It tries to manoeuvre and hence, can be manoeuvred. It tries to mesmerize and hence, can be mesmerized. It tries to program everything and hence, can be programmed. Whereas the kundalini does not try to dictate, impress, manoeuvre, mesmerize or program, and hence, cannot be bossed, impressed, manoeuvred, mesmerized or programmed.

The intellect projects in the future, but the future does not exist. It projects the future to seek returns, and as the returns diminish, it scraps its projections. The law of diminishing returns regards the elderly like medicine bottles whose date has expired. Inadvertently, it makes way for a 'use and throw' culture. We see people dying every day but the intellect does not tell us that we, too, will die, and hence, should not hang on to possessions. Cigarette packs carry a warning which states, 'smoking is injurious to health', but the intellect of the smoker turns a blind eye, because it seeks instant gratification. We watch drunkards fall out of pubs, but that does not stop the intellect from making a beeline to the bar. Children are sexually abused, but the intellect does not know that our children could be next.

Of course, the postmodern generation is far more aware of these issues. They aspire to be a better version of themselves through their intellect. But the direction of the intellect is linear, and after it reaches a dead end, it recoils back, much like the mental ideologies of socialism, communism, and capitalism recoiled. Perhaps, it is time to switch gears and connect to our kundalini. Rationality can be lured to take sides, but not our kundalini because she is the cutting edge of intelligence. Nor can she be mesmerized by wizardry because she is the power of absolute truth. Nor can she be seduced by the passion of erotica because she is the power of innocence.

She records everything like a tape recorder. For instance, when a thief steals, his kundalini records his misdeed. However, her point is not to find his faults but to empower him to overcome them. This finds resonance with Levi H. Dowling's akashic records:

> Unaided by the Spirit-breath, the work of intellect tends to solve the problems of things we see, and nothing more. The senses were ordained to bring into the mind mere pictures of the things that pass away; they do not deal with the real things; they do not comprehend eternal law. But man has something in his soul, a something that will tear the veil apart that he may see the world of real things. We call this something Spirit consciousness; it sleeps in every soul and cannot be awakened until the Holy Breath knocks at the door of every soul, but cannot enter until the will of man throws wide the door.

The Holy Breath is none other than the kundalini. While Levi points out the limitations of rationality, let us not forget its own usefulness. After the kundalini opens the sixth chakra, her light falls on our attention and integrates it with our rationality. As transformation occurs in our awareness, rationality becomes our friend and starts to guide us in the right direction. The kundalini bestows upon us a witness state.

If we witness how the spider spins its web and then gets caught in it, we can learn something from it—we witness the unseen hands that try to dig in our pockets. But we enjoy their ploy because we understand the stupidity behind it! We witness the myths of logic and enjoy the humor behind it! But more importantly, as we witness the dance of the waves and how they reach the shores, we learn how to reach the other side through the chaos of the world.

But wait, the witness state allows us to see one thing more—there cannot be any absolute value because we have not discovered the Absolute. Till then, everything is relative, and that is what creates the confusion between right and wrong.

There is only one way a flower can become a fruit, and that's the way of the living process. Once we become aware of the living process, we know the Absolute and the relative. Thereafter, the doubt between 'my way or your way' drops, and we silently witness the reality. Just as how, upon reaching the heart of an onion, it cannot be peeled further, in the witness state, as the layers of conditioning and ego peel off, it allows us to witness our blind spots and get the larger picture of our 'wholesomeness'. As we endeavour to engage in a relationship with our wholesomeness, it engenders us with a tenacity that is undaunted by the pressure of circumstances. Our tenacity enables us to keep ourselves above the mounting pressures of life, like a lotus that keeps itself above the water.

With the experience of our wholesomeness, we realize we are a part and parcel of the whole. Thereafter, we do not say 'who is the other'. The power of love is so great that with the movement of our fingers, we can move the kundalini of others. Whereas a lawyer's success depends on his argument skills, kundalini's awakening does not depend on any skills but on the Absolute point: she works through the living process. When the kundalini rises, she attracts the attention inside. When she touches the Spirit, the attention becomes enlightened. As our attention gets the light, we start feeling the blocks of a person's chakras like an X-ray. As we start feeling the kundalini, its nature and its position in others, we can help raise their kundalini; the love of our spirit starts acting. Without her love, it is difficult to help people and get them to see another way.

Each chakra within encodes a fundamental law of the living process. Any negation of its laws mirrors on the chakra and also on our fingertips. This is the experience of the living process, from seeds to stars, from atoms to galaxies, from microcosm to macrocosm. As one's recognition is established, the power of discrimination is attained. This is not the petty discrimination between black and white but a key that opens our mental blocks. Shri Mataji Nirmala Devi reveals, 'The pure intelligence is that which sees the game of this intellect and that which sees the limited function of rationality. Rationality is a limited thing. So, you have to jump into the space. When you are in the space, you are not in the capsule. But if you are in the capsule, you are not in the space.'

The past and the future keep flashing on the capsule's radar. The past is over and the future does not exist. But the mind is such a prankster, every time we try to close its file; it contrives to escape us! So, we have to look for a way to close the past unfinished files.

A futuristic person feels insecure because he is afraid of the uncertainties of the future. The future is uncertain because it does not exist, and hence, cannot be predicted by logic. On the other hand, the magnetic current of the past sucks our attention towards the traumas etched in the subconscious. However, when the kundalini rises, she has the greatest magnetic force of all and sucks our attention to the central channel—the present. The power of her love fills our cracks and forges the splits in our psyche. She is the winged power of transformation and harmonizes our mind with our spirit, and our consciousness with collective consciousness. The connection spontaneously reconciles us with our true nature—love. We realize that unconditional love is neither the past nor the future—it is the living process of the present. Moreover, it is greater than the truth because unconditional love is the giver of truth.

Our vision of the New Age world rests on the bedrock of collective consciousness. And that is only possible if we focus on the ascent of our kundalini. Our attention works like a laser beam and its efficiency depends on its sharpness. As the liver is the seat of attention, Zen masters, Sufi saints and Indian yogis spent lifetimes zealously guarding their liver against any detriment to their attention like alcohol, drugs, etc. As our attention comes into focus, wisdom is born. Our wisdom tells us that the most important product of knowledge is ignorance. The more we know, the more we do not know. Wisdom also allows us to see our mistakes and correct them, and that's all that matters!

> And our natural willingness to act
> is made weak by too much thinking,
> and actions of great urgency and importance
> because of this sort of thinking
> get thrown off course,
> and cease to be actions at all.
>
> —*Hamlet*, Act 3, Scene 1

13

THE PERENNIAL CONNECTION

Thou perceivest the Flowers put forth their precious Odours!
And none can tell how from so small a center comes such sweet,
Forgetting that within that Center Eternity expands...

—William Blake

What Blake envisioned as the expanse of eternity, Carl Jung envisaged as the universal unconscious. Because we are not conscious of this universal power, we call it the 'universal unconscious'. We are unconscious of it because it is not in our central nervous system. However, our evolutionary process remains incomplete till we achieve the state of collective consciousness. That is to say, till the universal unconscious registers on our central nervous system.

But how? By connecting to our kundalini because she is the missing link between our conscious mind and the universal unconscious.

As the golden shafts of the kundalini open the seventh chakra called the Sahasrara, it accelerates a jump in our consciousness. Atoms and molecules do not have the possibility to achieve absolute awareness but human beings do because when they get connected to the Spirit, they feel the all-pervading power of love. Before that, they do not feel it because

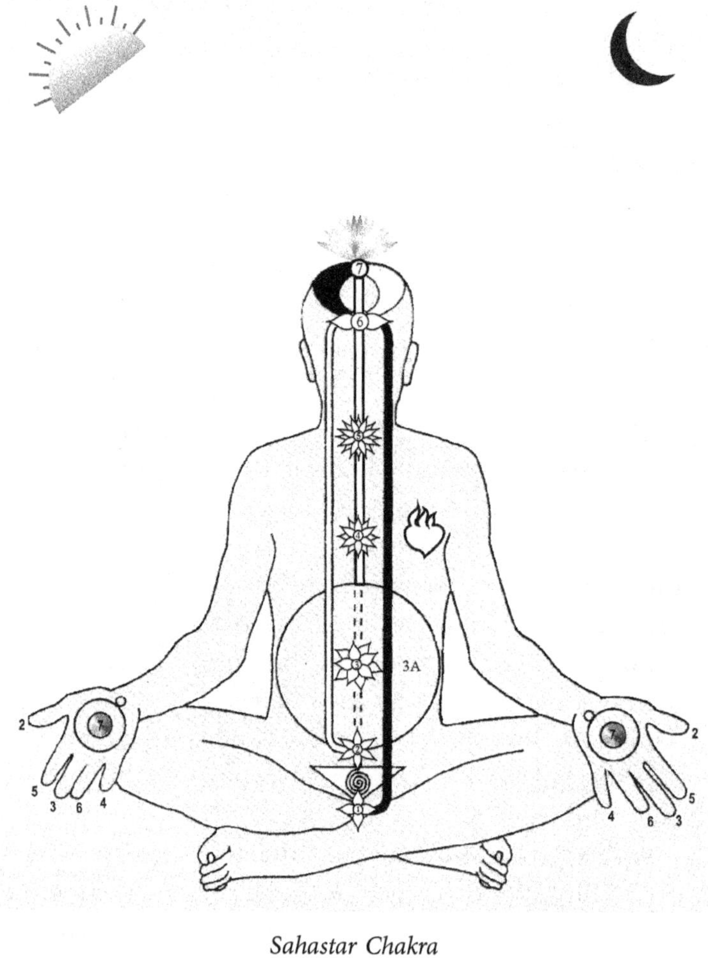

Sahastar Chakra

the one who feels it is the spirit. Like in a hall of mirrors, each mirror reflects the other mirror, and thus, the reflections become infinite; similarly, the love of the all-pervading power is reflected everywhere; on our central nervous system, in the atoms and molecules. It is not a hypothesis or a supposition, but one actually feels love for the others.

It is a spontaneous process like when a seed matures, it naturally sprouts. The only human effort involved is to put the seed into Mother Earth. When a realized soul awakens our kundalini, she flows like a river and steadily circumvents the huge rocks as she winds her way to the ocean. She gently soothes our anxieties and fears as she takes our boat across the sea of illusion. As our kundalini brings the world closer, we also become more seamless. However, a doubting mind may miss the boat!

> But the man who is ignorant, who has no faith, who is of a doubting nature, perishes. For the doubting soul there is neither this world nor the world beyond nor any happiness.
>
> —Bhagavad Gita 4:40

All the chakras subsume in the Sahasrara, the thousand-petalled lotus. The spirit resides in the heart, but has its seat in the corona of the thousand-petalled lotus. This is the place that the kundalini opens, the point of union or yoga at which the attention is united to the spirit, and unity takes place at all levels. Before the kundalini awakens, the energy of the chakras is limited; however, after the union, it becomes unlimited. For instance, water in a tank can stagnate or be finished, whereas spring water connected with an infinite source remains ever fresh and never finishes. It enables us to cull energy from an infinite source of creativity without being burnt out.

Unless we overcome the distortions in the human brain chakra, the chaos of this world is not going to die. However, no sooner than the kundalini comes home to the brain chakra, she functions like a GPS and thereby, helps us to navigate through the chaos of the world. Her GPS not only gives the best direction but also directs the best happenings our way! As the good happenings start reoccurring, it strikes us as a coincidence. But there is more to it than meets the eye! Lord Krishna called it 'Yoga Kshema', meaning that welfare follows after union with collective consciousness. On the surface, it appears to be a coincidence, but in reality, it is the working of cosmic intelligence. At a deeply fundamental level, the separate parts of the universe are connected in an infinite and immediate way through the vibrations of the Spirit. Albert Einstein pointed out, 'Everyone who is seriously involved in the pursuit of science becomes convinced that a Spirit is manifested in the laws of the universe—a Spirit vastly superior to man.' It is just to say the Spirit that manifests in the universe also reflects in human beings.

After all, as the Spirit reflects everywhere, our brain chakra and the cosmic brain chakra tune in to the same frequency. Thus, it's not so difficult for the human chakras to receive super-intelligence from the cosmic chakras. The receptors inbuilt in the chakras pick up the signals from the super-intelligence. Without going through the censorship of our intellect, our intellect beams information into our attention. In a sense, our chakras function like computers, and collective consciousness is the super-intelligence behind it. Thus, when the chakras are in sync, they reflect the primordial laws, philosophies, art, literature and science encoded in the collective consciousness. British mathematician Roger Penrose concluded that there must exist an external bank of data from which new knowledge is drawn out. Shri Mataji Nirmala Devi affirms, 'The whole social structure and laws came from the unconscious. The unconscious knows the divine laws but by the time they reach human beings, there are some distortions, but we go on improving.'

The distortions are obviously caused by the deliberations of the intellect. But after the kundalini is awakened, she configures the distortions and improves the receptivity of the chakras. Once the chakras are in sync, an artist churns out works beyond his imagination as though an unknown hand directs the strokes of his brush. Likewise, the founding fathers of the American constitution transfigured individual freedom to a height that humankind never knew existed, as though an unseen hand encoded the freedom of the Spirit in the constitution! Similarly, while Einstein played with soap bubbles, the unseen hand stumbled on the Theory of Relativity: 'From somewhere unknown, the theory of relativity dawned upon me.' The unseen hand also directed the poems of William Blake and of course, the thoughts of Mahatma Gandhi!

As we grow into thoughtless awareness, introspection ceases to be a mental activity. In thoughtless awareness, we get inspiration by which we know what is wrong without any analysis. Cosmic vibrations are conscious, and hence, work relentlessly to configure the distortions created by mental activity. Even before we plan, they work out everything for us at the appointed time because they love us very much. They are more aware of our needs than we are, and besides, they are far more efficient! As they take over all the planning, watching them churn simple solutions to complex problems is very relaxing. We say, 'Wow! What a miracle!' Of course, all the solutions are stored in our unconscious bank, but our busy mind fails to see it! In fact, the solutions exist in the problem but only after the kundalini enlightens the attention does our intuitive wisdom gets it!

But our conscious mind is not aware of our intuitive wisdom. Intuitive wisdom is not borrowed, superimposed or pirated; nor is it hybrid; it is original. It provides remarkable solutions to the most complex problems. To the weak, problems are stumbling blocks, but to a realized soul blessed with intuitive wisdom, they are stepping stones. Intuitive wisdom comes to us only in thoughtless awareness. Mahatma Gandhi recounted his experience of intuitive wisdom on the 19 March 1919, when he was devastated by the news of a Bill that ruthlessly put down all forms of patriotic activities as sedition.

> That night I fell asleep while thinking over the question. Towards wee hours of the morning I woke up somewhat earlier than usual. I was still in that twilight condition between sleep and consciousness when suddenly the idea broke upon me—it was as if in a dream…that we should call upon the country to observe a general strike on that day…let all people of India suspend their business on that day and observe the day as one of fasting and prayer.

The whole of India from one end to the other, towns as well as villages, observed a complete strike on 6 April. The total success of the strike took the British authorities completely by surprise. Intuitive wisdom churned out a technique mankind did not know existed.

The kundalini gives us access to the bank of intuitive

wisdom. The illusory nature of ego-identifications diminishes through the unchanging awareness of intuitive wisdom. As our attention reflects the infinite, we become the infinite, and as we become global, we think globally. We are concerned about global problems and seek global solutions through the eyes of our spirit.

To get a window on the Spirit, we have to, foremost, understand the nature of the Spirit. Her nature is complete awareness, and she is completely aware of her nature of love. She loves us more than we love ourselves. She is never aggressive, judgmental or dominating. She respects our freedom because only in our freedom is it possible for us to ascend. She is the humility and compassion of Christ, who washed his disciples' feet. She is the anguish of Mother Mary, who watched her son being crucified. And above all, she is the power of resurrection that forgives all that may have gone wrong, and thus, gives us our rebirth. Sufis described it as the union of the lover with his beloved.

In the words of Saint Jnanadeva:

> [The kundalini] retains its power until it is absorbed in the Supreme Brahman... Making itself steady in the 'Brahmarandhra', it spreads out its arms in the form of the notion—'I am the Supreme Brahman', [Absolute] and embraces the very Supreme Brahman. The screen of the five gross elements then gets dropped down and they both—the life-wind and the Supreme—meet together bodily, and it (wind) along with the sky absorbs itself into the Supreme Brahman getting one with it. Just as the sea-water becomes pure through the clouds (by the process of evaporation etc.), pours itself down into rivers and streams and then ultimately re-joins the sea, in the

same way, the individual soul, with the help of the human form, enters into the Supreme and secures, O Son of Pandu, union with it (just as sea-water).

[T]here then remains nothing like any 'object of knowledge' and whatever further might be said, would all be in vain. That stage from where words turn back, where all fancies and ideas get destroyed, where even the remotest touch or reach of thought cannot have any access, that stage... It is beginningless, limitless Supreme Spirit, and is verily the primary seed of the Universe, the ultimate goal of the Yoga-Study, and the very sentience full of bliss; all forms, the state of emancipation, all beginning and end are all uprooted there... Those that strive unflinching till the end, reach the form of the Self and secure the ultimate goal.

There then remains nothing like conquering the mind or any reliance on meditation. It is a self-conscious state in which one perceives the self-active power of the Supreme Spirit—the all-pervading power of Divine love whose essential nature is self-unfolding, self-delighting, Existence, Consciousness and Bliss.

—Jnaneshwari, 6.15

What Saint Jnanadeva described as the all-pervading power of Divine love is no different from what Jung called universal consciousness or collective consciousness. It should not be mistaken for a passive state because it is a dynamic force that changes the very genes of society. We realize that so far, whatever we believed was our conditioning. It was artificial. Whereas, in actuality, it is the living force that sprouts a seed and also that causes the heart to beat.

The beating of the heart emits vibrations of love that bond the human race. The skin colour may vary, but Guru Nanak said, 'Listen to the divine music that beats in every heart'. When we are lost in its music, time ceases to be important for us because it is for others. Everyone belongs to us and everything is ours, yet we are attached to nothing. Nor is the fragrance of individuality lost—on the contrary, it enhances the fragrance of the bouquet. A flower in the bouquet has no self-interest and only thinks of others.

For instance, during the Indian freedom struggle, the masses were inspired by the fragrance of Mahatma Gandhi, and they gathered in his bouquet. The fragrance of the bouquet became stronger and stronger after each ordeal. As they peered through the prism of his bouquet, they, too, saw the larger picture. The larger picture was none other than the working of the collective heart. Thus, they enjoyed a freedom they did not know existed. This inner freedom allowed them to enjoy their profession, be it an artist, weaver, carpenter, butcher, fisherman, businessman, politician or a warrior.

Thus, as a small pocket of a population plugs into the mains of collective consciousness, their positive vibrations form a caucus that positively transforms the society. Perhaps it can be observed more clearly in nature. For instance, farmers have discovered that their crop-yield enhanced manifolds when they vibrated the seeds before sowing. Moreover, the crop grew so resilient that fertilizers were not required. Thus, at the collective level, the resonance of vibrations has a cascading effect through morphic resonance.

In 1981, British biochemist Rupert Sheldrake discovered that the form, development and behaviour of living organisms are organized by invisible morphic fields that function across time and space. As a group of animals learn and behave a certain way, other groups in other parts of the world might develop the same skills. Thus, as the kundalini of large groups of people all over the world is ignited, the morphic resonance of their vibrations would transform the awareness of people across the world.

The Berlin Wall was not brought down by violence or politics, but by the morphic resonance of vibrations. The vibrations emanating from our spirit. Her vibrations resonate with everybody. As they resonate collectively, they transform the consciousness of our family, country and the world. It follows that, if we want world peace, there has to be peace within; there are no shortcuts. Thus, as vibrations penetrate our economy, politics, education, health, agriculture, ecology and science, it will fulfil every scientist's dream of the grand unification of all energies!

14

LOVING VIBRATIONS

There is no matter without vibrations.
Atoms and molecules have vibrations.
But all falsehood we have accepted stops vibrations.

—Shri Mataji Nirmala Devi

The cosmic vibrations dance rhythmically in various combinations, permutations and configurations choreographed by a living process. The vibrations of the tiniest microcell in the human body resonate with its joyful rhythm, but we are unaware of it. However, after self-realization, our nerves start emitting vibrations on our central nervous system and we become aware of resonance as unified cells in a collective body. The incarnations who felt the union shared their experience as cool vibrations. For instance, our Lord Jesus Christ described them as the 'cool wind of the Holy Ghost'. Adi Shankaracharya termed it as 'saleelamchaitanya', i.e. the cool breeze. According to Saint Jnanadeva, 'The life-wind emerges out of the kundalini and creates a cooling sensation in the body internally as also externally.'

Every human being has vibrations within their spirit, but they only manifest once realization is achieved. Cool vibrations

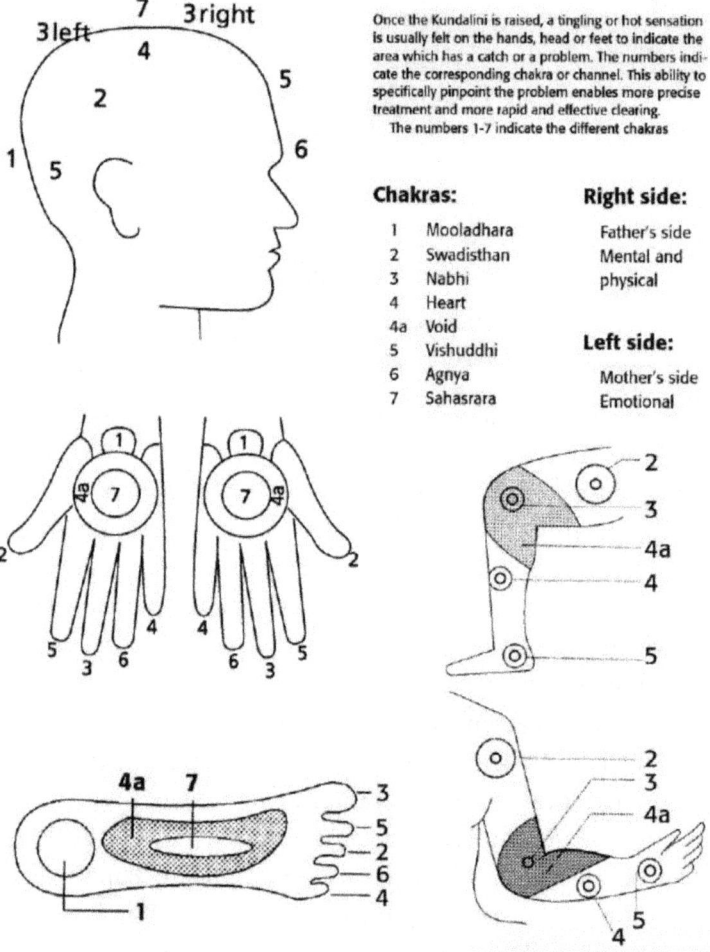

The position of the chakras on the hands, feet, limbs and the brain.

are felt atop the head and on the fingertips as the kundalini pierces the fontanel bone. According to Shri Mataji Nirmala Devi, the vibrations of the living process think, cooperate, cure, relate everything, report messages like telecommunication and above all, they love.

However, all the falsehood we have accepted in life hinders us from feeling their flow. Fortunately, after self-realization, the kundalini unblocks the chakras and directs the vibrations to cure the damaged chakras. Thus, after the first flood of vibrations, as the kundalini recedes to stitch the damaged chakras, we feel hot vibrations release on the palm of our hands.

Nonetheless, the working of the kundalini cannot be understood through the mind. In our mind, we live alone, whereas when we live in the spirit, we are no more alone; we become collective. Our consciousness expands into the collective consciousness. In the new dimension of collective consciousness, our kundalini helps us all the time without the deliberations of our conscious mind. She speaks to us through vibrations. For instance, if we think of something and the vibrations are cool, it is a positive signal. Conversely, hot vibrations indicate a negative signal. Positive vibrations wire us to the right people and right places for the right happenings at the right time. The sequences of life may not change, but for sure, the consequences change as things that did not work out earlier begin to come our way effortlessly. Furthermore, our stamina increases; not that the nature of the task changes but our ability to do it increases.

Thus, through this new vibratory awareness, we transcend the mind, our awareness becomes different, our priorities and values change—we become a new personality, we start

Vibrations are seen as streams of light above a gathering of Sahaja Yoga practitioners.

behaving differently, we take to things that are vibratory and auspicious, and we are not alone, bored or depressed because we feel the joy of our own spirit. Peace settles down and we begin to enjoy the state of collective love.

Having said that, let us not forget our transformation depends on how we harmonize the living process.

The new vibratory awareness guides us on how to harmonize with the living process and remain grounded in the world's chaos. It also enables us to observe what disrupts it. For example, if we are in the company of an individual or a group who emit hot vibrations, our vibrations send signals to our fingertips and alert us. Each finger is a meridian of a chakra. The moment it receives a negative signal, our centre-heart chakra instantly starts generating antibodies. As we protect the body from adverse weather, our chakras protect us from negativity. Not only does the metascience of Sahaja Yoga helps us feel vibrations and decode them, and teaches us how to use them to protect our chakras. Moreover, we know about ourselves, we also know about others—we feel their blocks and know how to ease them. Thus, it becomes possible to give realization to others without any difficulty by raising their Kundalini. Not just that, a seeker can be directed to improve his meditation by balancing his chakras.

Dr B. Bhattacharya, in his work *Science of Cosmic Ray Therapy*, states:

> The photograph of a person has the same set of vibrations as the person himself and therefore, the cosmic ray generated and focused at the photograph of the patient, instantaneously travels with its natural speed of light, and recognizes and envelopes the person concerned. This

cosmic ray immediately starts its work in the appropriate place within the person.

After realization, one gets vibrations like the cool breeze from Her Holiness Shri Mataji Nirmala Devi and even her photograph. This corroborates with Dr Bhattacharya's discovery that the photograph of a person has their vibrations. In this new vibratory awareness of Sahaja Yoga, it is possible to decode the problem from the person's photograph because every human being has got vibrations within his spirit, but they only manifest when he gains realization. Furthermore, his vibrations are the material carriers of the field of his chakras.

15

MEDITATION

The one who tastes, knows,
The one who tastes not, knows not,
Don't speak of heavenly beverage;
Offer it at your banquets and say nothing.
Those who like it will ask for more;
Those who don't aren't fit to drink it.
Close the shop of debate and mystery,
Open the teahouse of experience.

—Yusuf Hamadani, eleventh-century
Persian scholar and spiritual leader.

Meditation is an ambiguous grey zone that means different things to different people. The intent of the seeker may stretch from attaining therapeutic benefits to the realization of some spiritual concept. Unconsciously, it is aimed at becoming one with the Whole. The conception of that Whole may seem subjective, but it can be understood as the living process, or all-pervading energy, or collective consciousness, or God Almighty or the feminine principle.

We have read books on the subject, but how do we experience it? Meditation is the prescribed answer.

Sahaja Yoga meditation is a great way to experience it. By tuning into the frequency of one's own spirit, one experiences thoughtless awareness. The kundalini settles at the seventh chakra when all the chakras are in harmony. It enlightens the central nervous system, whereby we experience the joy of collective consciousness. Thus, meditation is effortless—in fact, it is organic.

According to Shri Mataji Nirmala Devi, 'How much you meditate means how much you love. You are transmitters of the waves of love. Everywhere you are sitting in meditation, you are transmitting vibrations.'

It follows that as our seventh chakra opens, it spreads waves of love during meditation, for without them, the seeker becomes cold and aloof. Thus, meditation is the spontaneous flow of unconditional love—the vibrations of love cannot be manufactured by visualization, daydreaming, covert self-instructional training, self-hypnosis or any other psychiatric-psycho-physiological-relaxation-curative therapy. It also implies that a meditation technique should not be predetermined, categorized or likely to result from habit, selective inattention or perception.

Shri Mataji reveals:

> The idea of meditation is not to sit down cross-legged for hours together, and to be lost to the world. I am in meditation all the time. When we are one with the spirit, we are in meditation all the time. I think all the trees are in meditation—they are one with the Whole. They do not know that they are in meditation but you will know that. That is the difference.

But if the 'part' loses its connection with the Whole, it plays into the hands of the mind, and is influenced by its moods. What determines these moods? If we are very agitated, our mind is restless and this reflects in our mood. These moods deflect thoughts from the ego or superego—the Spirit has no moods. When we shut our eyes to meditate, our thoughts race about like mice on steroids. If we allow the thoughts to pass, we will observe a space between two thoughts. The vibrations of the kundalini go on widening this space till the thoughts stop and we experience thoughtless awareness. But this is not an empty space—it is filled with the joy of the Spirit.

The Spirit uplifts our mood. Before the kundalini awakens, we may suffer from the past hangover. For instance, a shock or a tragedy may have left an inescapable imprint on our subconscious. The more we dwell upon it, the more we feel its pain. By reliving the tragedy, we develop a melancholic nature. Our inherent nature is the same as the Spirit, i.e. joy, whereas our second nature is the mind. It is acquired. Likewise, childhood sufferings may have left an imprint in our second nature from where our fears, traumas and old-age eccentricities generate, but our kundalini empowers us to fix them. She smoothes the dents and angularities surfacing from the past by spreading her vibrations in various rhythmic mandala-like movements. Thus, by silencing the mind, the kundalini leads us into a state of thoughtless awareness. According to Shri Mataji Nirmala Devi:

> For a second go into thoughtlessness and when you take decisions you will take such decisions which are not in the likes of many—dynamic...absolutely dynamic! The

worry, fear, anger, servility, slavishness, inferiority and all complexes will all fall away.

For sure, the deepest and most meaningful language of all is the language of silence. The silence of the spirit is none other than the inner silence or 'shunya' of Buddha, the 'nirvana' of Mahavira, the 'moksha' of Vedanta and the 'kingdom of heaven' of Christ. As our kundalini puts our minds in a silent mode, we enjoy inner peace. Not just that: as we become peaceful, we radiate peace towards others. Having said that, let us not mistake the 'peaceful mode' for a state of trance or passive, unconscious perception. When the actualization of the peaceful mode happens, we silently enjoy the beautiful orchestra conducted by an unseen conductor. Its notes come from the unchanging reality that is beyond any notion of existence or its negation, speculation or imagination. We cannot think about it—it is an actualization of our central nervous system like the sprouting of a seed. However, though the sprouting of a seed is spontaneous, the gardener has to look after the tender sapling. In the same way, a seeker has to look after his self-realization in the beginning. As he is living a normal life with a regular job, he must become aware of the problems caused by his blocked chakras by understanding the proper decoding system and its Sahaja practices.

Often, the consciousness that 'I am giving vibes (vibrations)' deceives us into believing that we are the doer. The 'I' consciousness creates ripples of mental anxiety that gains alarming proportions. In the state of anxiety, the vital link of the part with the Whole snaps, and the recovery of the individual is dependent on the limited energy supply of the sympathetic nervous system. If the energy of the sympathetic nervous system is corroded, the individual fails to recover. Sahaja Yoga meditation facilitates recovery by re-establishing the vital link to the mains. Its prism changes the way we look at things. It allows us to notice things—it has little to do with the things we see, and everything to do with the way we see them.

When transformation takes place within you, you become so empowered that nothing can dominate you.

> No habits can dominate you.
> No guru can dominate you.
> No idea or fixation can dominate you.
> Your attention becomes enlightened.

> —Shri Mataji Nirmala Devi

Clinical Findings of Sahaja Yoga Meditation

Meditative Sleep

When the kundalini settles in the sahasrara (limbic) area of the brain, the attention does not shift to thoughts coming from the area of the subconscious. The sleep is very deep and the person wakes up completely refreshed. The duration of the sleep may be short, but the batteries recharge swiftly through a smooth uninterrupted connection to the living process. If this connection is maintained throughout the day, there is no tiredness.

Meditation at the Agnya Chakra

Concentrating on the point between the eyebrows is dangerous as it overloads the chakra and damages it. People who are clairvoyant get side-tracked into seeing the supernatural that is of no interest to the kundalini or evolution. Instead of ascending, such people go off on tangents that hamper their evolution. Instead, one should keep one's attention on the kundalini above one's head.

Clinical Experiments

Most experiments on varied meditation groups have revealed that the practice of meditation is accompanied by a decrease in neuroticism, depression, anxiety, irritability and hypertension. It increases self-control, self-actualization and happiness. According to Prof. U.C. Rai, 'The control of stress factors by drugs like tranquilizers has been in use in spite of their side effects and habit-forming nature. However, it is not a satisfactory long-term answer to tackle the problem of severe stress. Hence, various relaxation techniques, meditation, etc. have been tried to reduce the effect of stress on the body.'[*]

In 1970, Shri Mataji Nirmala Devi demonstrated that Sahaja Yoga is easy to practise, and, is, in fact, spontaneous and effortless:

> It is based on an internal technology. The perception of cool breeze from the palm to the top of the head confirms the awakening of the kundalini. After the awakening of the kundalini, one goes into a stage of self-realization and thoughtless-awareness—a blissful stage with profound relaxation of body and mind. In this communication,

---

[*]Publication on scientific studies on the effect of Sahaja Yoga on the human body and mind and its role in preventing stress disorders published in the *Journal International Medical Science Academy (JIMSA)* Vol. 2, March 1988 by Prof. U.C. Rai, former head of the Department of Physiology, Sucheta Kriplani Hospital, New Delhi.

some effects of Sahaja Yoga on heart rate, blood pressure, galvanic skin resistance, blood lactic acid and urinary vanillyl mandelic acid have been studied so as to define the role of Sahaja Yoga in stress.

Research by Dr Deepak Chugh and Dr Sandeep Sethi produced the following results:

> In conclusion, Sahaja Yoga practice produces significant physiological changes in both the trainees and advanced Sahaja Yogis by bringing about equilibrium between sympathetic and parasympathetic responses. It knocks down the sympathetic dominance that is usually seen in situations of stress. Thus, Sahaja Yoga helps an individual in providing relief against stress.[*]

Meditation and Psychoanalysis

Dr Rustom Burjorjee, a psychiatrist based in the UK, said:

> It is generally accepted that the universe is composed of maya or illusion which conceals the absolute nature of the Self and makes possible the existence of a diversified field and differentiated creation. It is this differentiation and diversification that makes possible the existence of the human personality, the field of the practice of psychoanalysis. If this delusion were to vanish through pure yoga, then there would be no personality and no psychoanalysis. Conversely, psychoanalysis

---

[*] 'Effects of Sahaja Yoga Practice on patients of Psychosomatic diseases' and 'Physiological Effects of Kundalini Awakening by Sahaja Yoga', by Dr Deepak Chugh and Dr Sandeep Sethi.

by perpetuating the myth of the ego and individual conditioning, which forms personality, may block yoga since the two are enemies of each other.

Yoga essentially means union—union of the individual with the absolute through his own Atma or Spirit with the Absolute or Paramatma—a spiritual cosmic lord. The individual who has not this connection cannot meditate, for how can one meditate on something one knows not?

In the absence of this connection it follows that in so called 'meditation' the awareness must be caught in something other than the absolute self. What is this?

The universe is believed to be replete and overflowing with products of delusion and one of these is the individual personality—the field of study of psychoanalysis. In the absence of enlightenment or yoga, this will lead to further and further entanglement in delusion leading to what can be called 'bharanti jalam' or the net of illusion.

The essence of enlightenment or yoga is to take someone out of the net of illusion and to give him detachment from life—so that whatever his existence, he remains detached from it—in the language of the Gita, to be beyond the dualities of experience. To such a soul psychoanalysis is irrelevant—since the positioning of a mode of action is negated. In detachment all things are the same. Yoga postulates the importance of existence and awareness/attention over action. Whatever one is aware of is more important than what is done by or to one, and this is done by the immediate dissolution of the individual in the absolute.

The attainment of yoga is only possible through

the intervention of an enlightened or realized soul as of the Divine itself, and consists of the awareness of the Divine. Hence, from these few words, it follows there is no connection between yoga and psychoanalysis.

16

HOW TO SEEK THE TRUTH

At the very outset, we have to understand that we cannot create truth, we cannot organize truth. Truth is what it is. We cannot cheat truth. We have to reach that point to receive it. It is not a mental achievement. It is not a concept. We cannot change it. Sahaja Yoga establishes the proof of truth and enables you to experience it. Where the seekers of truth are misled, the results have been disastrous.

—Shri Mataji Nirmala Devi

Often, seekers are unaware that their spiritual aspirations are hijacked by false gurus. Most psychic, spiritual and supraconscious groups are like drugs—they entice and entrap the seekers. In the circumstances of confusion, the cunning profits, and we miss out on the truth.

Hence, before we plunge into seeking powers, we should beware that not all powers contribute to a righteous path. Visions, voices, astral projection, auras, levitation, predictions and communications with the dead are all possible, but they do not lead to Truth. They empower us temporarily. They make our ego believe that we are special. But all these powers soon cause illness, distress and depression. They are clear invitations for spirit possession. They are detours that confuse, if not destroy, our true seeking. Rumi advises, 'I have been a seeker and I still am, but I stopped asking the books and the stars. I started listening to the teachings of my soul.'

The need to belong to a group or a community is normal. But some groups are after our money, others are after our spirit.

Despite all these conclusions, we did not give up their search. Before trusting a guru or seeking groups, if we are mindful of certain questions, we will not miss the signs posted on the crossroads:

- Is money taken at any time? The Truth cannot be owned, nor can it be bought or sold.
- Does the teacher use pressure techniques like salesmen? One should know the value of their path by one's own conviction, not by the number of books read, classes attended, or pledges made. Truth is not dependent upon salesmanship.
- Do we ourselves feel the effect of the technique? Do not be satisfied by the vague promise that we will be in an 'inner circle' at some time in the future.
- Do they clothe the followers in unusual dresses, seat them in strange postures, or submit them to wild chanting? The Truth is not something that has to be attained through strenuous efforts. It is the purity of our desire that counts, not the harshness of their tests.
- Is this a balanced path similar to that followed by the sages, yogis and great men of the past, or will it lead to frightening experiences of a subconscious or supraconscious nature?
- Are the members of the organization, including

the guru or leader, people one can trust? Are we comfortable with them? Do they display love and joy? Is their warmth genuine? Is the value of what they are teaching evident in their eyes?
- Is there freedom of choice to leave or continue? Follow the heart, not the ego. If there are fears or misgivings, give them heed. If in doubt and under duress, leave. Do not be bullied.
- Is there a way to verify how the system works? Whatever phenomenon occurs, the working of its principle should be ascertainable.
- Even if enlightenment is promised in any place of worship, be it a temple, mosque, church or meditation centre, what good would it do if we lack the desire to transform? We should introspect—what is it that brings us to these places?
- Introspect on conditioning. 'Do we subscribe to a religious faith because we were raised that way?'
  To de-brand ourselves, we must ask, 'Who am I?'
  Affirmation: 'I am who I am because of who we all are.'
  Next question: 'Who are we?'
  'Are we this body, mind, conditioning or ego?'

According to Einstein, the body is nothing but mass, and mass and energy are convertible. The mind, conditioning and ego are nothing but the products of our identification with the body mass. Consciousness is always singular, whereas the ego presents duality. Hence, we are pure consciousness. But the degree of our consciousness is limited—we have to achieve absolute consciousness. In the end, it is a personal journey and a personal choice, and no organization can possibly do the job for us. Once our kundalini is triggered, our consciousness starts transforming quietly until it reaches a stage where it becomes unstoppable.

17

STRESS BUSTERS

We know that plants die from lack of water, so we end up over-watering or, in other words, over-worrying about them. Poor things—this kills them too! The fact is that it's not just the plants—*we* over-worry too.

A worried husband could not fall asleep at night. As he turned and tossed, his wife shook him, 'What's the matter, honey?'

He answered, 'I owe $10,000 to my colleague. I promised to deliver it in the morning, but I don't have the money.'

The wife called the colleague, 'Sorry, John. My husband won't be coming to office today.'

Thereafter, the couple slept like a log but the worry-bug kept John tossing and turning!

It is a generally accepted scientific theory that human beings are social animals, and are empowered with intellectual capabilities, which constantly influence them to better their way of living. Of course, we should aspire to be a better version of ourselves in every possible way. The sun channel on the right side of sympathetic nervous system allows us to do just that—it empowers us to think, plan, speculate, imagine and dream of settling on the moon. Of course, it is not forbidden to dream! Unfortunately, animals can't because they are not gifted with the tool of imagination. However, this tool of imagination accomplishes one more function: it causes a mutation in our consciousness that gets on our last nerve—stress.

We should bear in mind that if animals are not stressed, why are humans stressed? Perhaps, as we imagine what does not exist, our galloping imagination conjures all kinds of fears and anxieties. Our thoughts carry our fears and anxieties. Thoughts flow either from the past or the future—there are no thoughts in the present. If there are no thoughts, there is no one to carry the anxiety. Hence, anxiety exists in the mind, and if there is no mind, there is no anxiety. It is just to say that anxiety comes from the sympathetic nervous system, but not from the parasympathetic nervous system. For instance, a motorist is stressed by traffic jams, a student is stressed by exams, a graduate is stressed by unemployment, a businessman is stressed by income tax, a salesman is stressed by a sales target, production managers are stressed by production targets and a housewife is stressed by the guests coming to dinner, etc. It is not the guests coming to dinner that stresses the housewife—it is the way she perceives her control over her guests. In medical terms, her stress can be viewed as a psychosomatic phenomenon. Psychosomatic medicine recognizes that many diseases and disorders are directly related to our behaviour. In other words, when out of balance, we are responsible for many of our own physical and emotional misfortunes; we need to regard the human being as a whole. We are just not asthmatic or alcoholic. We do not just suffer from angina or hypertension as an isolated physical or mental incident, but as part of the whole process of being a human being. There are reasons for these malfunctions and in simplistic terms, it boils down to imbalances; imbalances, whether physical, mental or emotional, spell trouble.

Hence, stress is not caused by just the guests coming to dinner, but any event can arouse a challenging and threatening reaction. Different people perceive situations differently and hence, have different reactions. For instance, the 'can't-bear-noise-people' cannot sleep in the slightest noise because there is already too much noise inside their Agnya Chakra. On the other hand, if our Agnya Chakra is peaceful, sound does not disturb, and we can enjoy sound sleep even on a railway platform. People relax while listening to their favourite song but go nuts at the sound of a neighbour's hammering. But the same sound could be music to a carpenter's ear! The tolerance limit differs from person to person, depending upon the state of one's chakras. Those with strong chakras can deal with higher stress levels while those with weak chakras suffer enormously even under modest amounts of pressure. Given a similar situation, some are more stress-prone than others. In a layman's language, when a material is subjected to load, the material gets stressed. For instance, if a cart is overloaded, it buckles under the weight. Thus, how we deal with the overload depends on the resilience and adaptability of our chakras.

The resilience and adaptability to face challenges can be compared to the flexibility of a rubber band—if it is stretched beyond its limits, it breaks. Likewise, a person's flexibility depends on how far his chakras can stretch within their tolerance limits. If it is stretched beyond their limit, they lose their mobility to release the hot vibrations, and thus, the negative vibrations spread to the corresponding organs, and surface in physiological and psychological symptoms like muscle tensions, indigestion, insomnia, obesity, high blood pressure, anger and depression. The continual imbalances in the chakras created by prolonged unabated stress generate ulcers, cardiovascular problems and cancer.

Many turn to alcohol, drugs and tranquillizers because they are unable to deal with stress. But instead of solving the problem, these escape routes fuel addiction. The abnormal stimulation triggers a state of emergency in the sympathetic nervous systems that propel the chakras to liberate more energy. Depending on the drug's potency, the additional flow of the energy engenders a feeling of relaxation, floating or hallucinations. However, the energy supply of the chakras is limited. As drug stimulation drains them, they draw energy from the other chakras. As the rising demand stretches the chakras beyond their limit, they relapse.

A world of increased aspirations and a highly competitive environment, combined with the phenomenon of receding resources, pushes the individual against the wall. He works under tremendous challenges without being sure of the results of his efforts. It is an irreversible reality from which there is no running away. The World Health Organization had predicted that stress would become the number one killer in the world by 2020. Recent surveys reveal that five times as many youths have stress compared to 10 years ago.

The physiology department of the Lady Hardinge College and the Sucheta Kriplani Hospital have established, through elaborate scientific studies, the effects of Sahaja Yoga on the human body and mind, and its role in preventing stress disorders. The study, published in the *Journal International Medical Sciences Academy (JIMSA)*, establishes that practising Sahaja Yoga for just a few weeks reduces tensions, and leads to deep relaxation of body and mind. Based on the experiments, the physiology department, in collaboration with the Defence Institute of Physiology and Applied Science, has done further research on the effects of Sahaja Yoga on epilepsy. As the patient's chakras are balanced, his drug dosage is reduced. Furthermore, the introduction of Sahaja Yoga in drug rehab centres worldwide has shown positive results. It has also been introduced in jails for rehabilitating inmates.

Indeed, as we connect to our inbuilt energy of the kundalini, it brings the chakras back to their axis and enables them to deal with stress without any medication. People who overthink stretch their mind beyond faith or hope and do not know how to deal with the stress in their chakras. However, after the awakening of the kundalini, the seeker knows how to apply the vibrations of the kundalini to release the stress from the chakras and vitalize them. With vibrations, the chakras expand their auras; as their circle becomes bigger, it engulfs both its sides and returns to its axis. As the cells start receiving information from the axis, they resume normal activity. Thus, as a person comes in the centre, sound no more disturbs him and he can sleep anywhere.

Stressed Mooladhara Chakra

The quality of innocence bestowed by the Mooladhara Chakra gives joy and is relaxing. For instance, the innocent smiles of children open our hearts, and their innocent pranks fill the home with laughter. On the other hand, thinking of sex all the time, watching obscene visuals or pornography overexcites the Mooladhara Chakra. The moon channel sucks the negative vibrations from the Mooladhara Chakra and parcels them to the optic chiasm at the Agnya Chakra, where it manifests in a roving eye. A roving eye spoils the attention, and instead of enjoying reality, it lusts for 'sex appeal' in everything. As 'sex appeal' is nothing but a mental projection, it does not get rewarded. In the absence of joy, the desiring force in the moon channel generates a mutation in the psyche of the Mooladhara Chakra—frustration—a phenomenon unknown to occur in any other species! The 'frustration drive' fuels rape and child abuse cases. The World Health Organization classifies 'compulsive sexual behaviour' as a mental disorder. At the physical level, prolonged periods of sexual excitement dry the petals of the chakra, causing impotency.

Stressed Swadhisthana Chakra

The second chakra empowers the seat of attention—the liver. The liver breaks down fat particles in the abdomen to replenish the grey and white cells in the brain. Much like a steam engine, it generates energy for the brain activity of thinking, planning and creativity. But as workaholics drive the engine beyond its capacity, it blows a fuse. Thus, it hampers the removal of toxins from the bloodstream. The toxins collected in the bloodstream slow down the distribution of nutrients to the organs and thereby impair their efficacy. Like a chimney, the sun channel sucks out the hot vibrations from the liver and bellows it to the chakras above. According to research done by Dr Deepak Chugh, Department of Physiology, Lady Hardinge Medical College, the surge of hot vibrations in the fourth and the fifth chakras constrict the lungs and the heart, leading to respiratory disorders like asthma:

> The experimental group C consisted of nine female asthma patients trained in Sahaja Yoga and followed up

for 16 weeks. Control group D consisted of nine female asthma patients of similar ages and socio-economic class who did not practise Sahaja Yoga meditation. Group C registered a significant improvement in lung function, and a significant decrease in the number of acute asthmatic attacks. As the clinical condition of the patients in group C improved, it was possible for all but one of them to cease all medication.

No significant changes were observed in the control group D. In Sahaja Yoga terms, asthma is said to be due to a constriction in the cardiac centre on the right side. A prediction of this hypothesis is that heat will accumulate in the liver due to the constriction blocking its upward movement.

The study further found that Sahaja Yoga awakens the kundalini, and thereby produces a state of thoughtless awareness with deep relaxation.

Chug's research also shows that hypertension occurs due to excessive right side sympathetic activity. In other words, hypertension occurs due to an imbalance between the moon and the sun channel. The sympathetic and parasympathetic systems act on the chakra, but in opposition to each other. The parasympathetic relaxes the chakras, increasing their vitality, whereas, the sympathetic constricts them, consuming their vitality. By activating the kundalini, the parasympathetic activity can be maximized and a balance is established. In addition, a change of awareness takes place such that the chakras can be felt both in the body and the hands. Thus, the patient gains a crystal clear understanding of his stress by reviving the vitality of his chakras. Likewise, the chakras of others can also be felt and brought into balance.

Research conducted on stressed children by Dr Linda Harrison, Royal Women Hospital, Sydney, showed considerable improvement in the children within just six weeks after them being introduced to Sahaja Yoga meditation. The cause of stress varied from exam syndrome and the parental pressure to overachieve. Meeting the expectation of the parents was known to drive some children to die by suicide.

After Sahaja Yoga meditation was introduced in government schools under the Maharashtra Education Board, Himachal Education Board and Delhi Education Board, there was a considerable decline in children's stress levels. Furthermore, as their Swadishthan Chakra cooled, their attention improved, and they were more engaged in their classwork and learning.

Stressed Nabhi Chakra

What do long working hours, traffic jams, panic and beating deadlines have in common with the nabhi chakra?

On the right side of the body, the sun channel sucks the hot vibrations from the liver and bellows them to the chakras above. Likewise, on the left side of the body, the moon channel sucks the hot vibrations from the brain and bellows them to chakras below. The nabhi bears the major brunt of the hot vibrations. The hot vibrations stress the stomach cells and cause them to secrete the stress hormone, cortisol. The secretion of the hormone cortisol increases the acid levels in the stomach. It causes ulcer formation and irritable bowel syndrome. There's a memorable scene in the film *Manhattan*, where Diane Keaton breaks up with Woody Allen, and wants to know why it isn't making him angry. The actor replies, 'I don't get angry—I grow a tumour instead!'

It gives us a window into the minds of those people who thrive on stress. They exude stress in their nature, behaviour and attitude, and as if that is not enough, the vibrations of their stressed chakras stress the chakras of not only human beings who come in their contact but also animals.

Recent research led by Lina Roth, Linköping University, Sweden, found that when dog owners go through a stressful period, they're not alone in feeling the pressure—they transfer it to their dogs. The patterns of cortisol levels in the hair of dog owners closely matched those found in their dogs. Thus, the owners influenced the dogs rather than the other way around. The same is true for plants. Plants absorb the vibrations of their owners, and their stress levels impair their growth.

Conversely, the loving vibrations of a realized soul can calm the chakras of those who come in contact with it. For instance, during the Partition riots in Bengal, the presence of Mahatma Gandhi worked like a soothing balm that miraculously abated the hate tsunami that had killed thousands. Of course, the chakras draw their vibrations from none other than the supreme source of love, kundalini.

More recently, research by Stanford University found an 18.9 per cent drop in anti-Muslim hate crimes in Merseyside in the period since the Egyptian Football icon Mohamed Salah signed for Liverpool in 2017. Thus, the vibrations of his peaceful chakras spread to the audience.

At the physical level, the nabhi chakra regulates the functioning of the spleen. The spleen is the speedometer of the body and as we press the accelerator to beat the deadline, it become agitated. It tries to meet the emergency by churning out more blood cells. In the state of chronic emergency, it ceases to secrete insulin. It is worrisome how younger people under 40 years are being increasingly diagnosed with diabetes.

The nabhi chakra bestows upon us the quality of contentment. A contented nabhi chakra engenders peace, but if the turmoil of thoughts arises, we lose out on the contentment. Turmoil generates an artificial hunger and leads to overeating. The hunger of the body can be satisfied by food, but the mind's hunger cannot be satisfied. Endless wanting throws the nabhi chakra into spasms.

A child delights in new toys, but new remains so only for a day, and then, what next? According to the law of physics, wants, in general, cannot be satisfied. Those who don't have money run after it, and also, the 'haves' do the same thing—the more they have, the more they want. If money could buy contentment, then the rich would be the most content! But on the contrary, they are the most stressed. Neither a lot more money nor more food is the recipe for a stressed nabhi chakra. Nor is miserliness the answer. On the contrary, thinking of money all the time raises stress levels. The nabhi chakra can be satisfied with very little or even the moon itself may not be enough for an irate one. Advanced studies found that despite rising incomes, people worldwide are feeling increasingly pressed for time—which undermines well-being, productivity, creativity, increased anxiety, insomnia, and was a critical factor in rising obesity rates. A stressed nabhi chakra throws the digestive system in a tizzy and renders it vulnerable to allergies.

However, new social allergies have come with the digital age. Certain behavioural patterns turn people off, like other people's children crying on a flight, delays, waiting in a queue etc.

Stressed Heart Chakra

A recent health study of inmates in a mental asylum revealed that their hearts continued to be robust though there were disorders in their brain functioning. As an overloaded cart buckles under its weight, likewise, an overworked heart chakra buckles under the brain-load. When the aggressive vibrations of the brain completely cover the heart chakra, the person experiences burnout. More than half the doctors in the US experience burnout at a rate that's twice as high as the average American worker's. According to a study published in the *Annals of Internal Medicine*, burnout costs US \$4.6 billion each year. 'The costs of burnout are related to doctors leaving health systems and working reduced hours. Burnout is generally defined as long-term stress linked to work.'

The World Health Organization defines burnout as, 'A syndrome conceptualized as resulting from chronic workplace stress that has not been successfully managed.'

It characterized the burnout syndrome in three dimensions:

- feelings of energy depletion or exhaustion;
- increased mental distance from one's job, or feelings of negativity or cynicism related to one's job;
- reduced professional efficacy.

The emotional intelligence of a balanced heart chakra knows how to deal with burnout syndrome. But if it gets clouded by the ego, its petals lose recourse to its intelligence. Bereft of emotional intelligence, the petals of the heart chakra close, leaving the person disconnected and depressed. We should bear in mind that depression is not the same thing as grief. Grief is a feeling that comes from losing a dear one.

At the loss of our dear ones, we feel sad and not depressed. Grief means the presence of love, whereas depression is an emptiness devoid of love. Small issues appear threatening and one makes a mountain out of a molehill. Acute depression causes withdrawal symptoms that lead to suicidal tendencies.

Furthermore, insecurities can fuel incurable diseases of which we are not aware. No doubt the petals of the heart chakra generate antibodies for the body's immune system. But under stress, their signals get blurred, which impairs the immune system's efficacy. When our defence mechanism grows weak, an alien entity that is not friendly to our heart chakra penetrates. Let's consider the cosmos as patterns of vibrations oscillating at different frequencies. We must bear in mind that all kinds of entities form these patterns. For instance, the human mass is bonded together by the Spirit that resides in the heart chakra. When any entity oscillating in the cosmos is not friendly to the harmonious functioning of the Spirit, it attempts to disrupt its functioning by feeding upon it like a parasite. An unfriendly entity that penetrates the heart chakra may seriously paralyse its functioning.

Stressed Vishuddhi Chakra

While the sixth chakra gets clouded by guilt, the stress levels rise. As the person does not know how to deal with it, he vents his stress in aggression, substance abuse, etc. He projects the guilt on others by finding their faults. But, if he is criticized, he recedes into his shell.

Another common escape route is obsessive behaviour such as smoking. But a smoker is not content to smoke by himself. He cannot help sharing his stress with others and as the Vishuddhi Chakra is the gateway to communication, the stress becomes viral.

After the kundalini's awakening, the vibration of our workplace becomes transparent. Where the vibrations are cool, the health and productivity of the workforce are far more positive than where the vibrations are hot. The same is true of clinics, hospitals, children's crèches and eateries.

Of course, the chakra could also be stressed by toxic cocktails. We are one body—a problem in one part affects the whole body. Even if only one chakra has caught it, the negativity affects all the chakras.

Stressed Agnya Chakra

At the intersection of the moon and the sun channel, a busy Agnya Chakra not only tries to control its own two channels, but also tries to control the channels of others, and, in the process, absorbs their stress. The golden rule is—what stresses you, controls you. Perhaps, we are not even aware of how much space in our bag of worries is taken away by other people's worries! Rather than controlling others, if we learn to control our thoughts, we could empty our Agnya Chakra, much like Little Bo Peep, who felt she had to go find her sheep and experienced some trauma in the process, only to realize the fault was her own and nothing had really happened to the sheep. Sometimes, this works for situations in our lives as well, and makes us realize that stress is all in the mind.

But if we go beyond the mind, it is possible to go beyond the stress. As the kundalini rises, she comes between the thoughts and places us in a stress-free zone of thoughtless awareness beyond the mind. As we step back and witness through the prism of the stress-free zone, we can see the rising and falling of thoughts without getting involved in their play. As we witness their play, we avoid being entangled in traumatic things, and thus, manage to survive the tensions of the world and reach the other side.

Of course, this never goes to say that we shouldn't be caring and loving, but we should do this with a detached concern rather than feeling over-worried or over-responsible.

The Agnya Chakra takes care of the optic chiasm that looks after the eyes at the physical level. The glare of the computer screen, the intensity of light emitted and its reflection results in excessive strain on the eyes and cumulatively causes:

- computer vision syndrome;
- chronic backache;
- blurred vision;
- mental stress;
- pink patches on the eyes;
- arthritis in the arm joint;
- cervical spondylitis.

The World Health Organization also recognizes video gaming as an addiction, listing it alongside gambling and drugs like cocaine.

Recently, a 16-year-old student suddenly became agitated while playing a video game on his mobile phone for four hours at a stretch. He started shouting, before he collapsed on the floor and died. The cardiologist who examined him stated, 'The excitement of the video game might have caused a surge in adrenaline, causing increased heart rate and cardiac arrest.'

The second chakra regulates the function of the kidneys and the adrenaline glands. The adrenaline rush is the way the body's defence mechanism works to combat stress. In a stressful situation, the adrenaline glands release the hormone adrenaline. Adrenaline is responsible for the fight-or-flight reaction to a threat or as a response to stress. The release of adrenaline in the body occurs very quickly, usually within a few seconds. It can make the body send extra oxygen to the lungs to aid a person to run away or it can increase the heart rate.

The chakras interact in various permutations and combinations, as in the above-mentioned case of burnout, the second chakra came to the rescue of the stressed sixth chakra. Thus, the network of the chakras is an interdependent relationship—they respond to each other, cooperate and help each other to beat stress. Stress in one chakra may surface elsewhere as in the burnout case, where the root cause of stress emanated at the Agnya Chakra, but the heart chakra bore its brunt. Hence, stress management cannot be exclusive to a particular chakra, but has to be inclusive of both the sympathetic systems—the moon and the sun channel.

Overactivity of the sympathetic nervous system leads to tensions, sleeplessness and other health problems caused by the constricted plexuses that are drained of energy. When the extraction falls too heavy on the chakras, they get separated from the Whole and move away from their axis. The axis gives guidance and a sense of proportion to the cells—how much to grow and how to coordinate. If the cell starts working on its own, it becomes malignant.

As the parasympathetic nervous system provides the antidote to the over-extraction of the sympathetic nervous system, Sahaja Yoga suggests an alternative drug-free physiological paradigm to combat stress. It does not treat each chakra exclusively, but rather treats the total sympathetic system inclusively, with the vibrations of our residual force, the kundalini.

18

GREEN FINGERS

Every seed which is sprouted has a small little primula, out of which comes out the shoot and the root. And the root is so delicate and small. At the tip of the root, there is a very intelligent cell and this cell knows how to carry on its journey. So it gradually penetrates into soft, muddy land, but when it comes across any stone, it encircles around it. Now, it could manage just avoiding it, but no! It encircles, so he uses that stone to support the tree in the future. So intelligent it is, and that's how it works out its way to the source of water.

—Shri Mataji Nirmala Devi

The intelligence at the tip of the seed comes from its indwelling kundalini. The blueprint of the big tree is inbuilt in the tiny seed. But something has to happen for the seed to sprout—it cannot sprout by itself. Its potential has to be connected to the magnetic field of Mother Earth for her kundalini to help sprout the seed. The living process of Mother Earth acts on the potential of the seed and causes it to sprout.

Similarly, vibrations are a living process—they act on the seed's potential to make it dynamic. It is just to say that if seeds are treated with vibrations, they become dynamic and

The kundalini of Mother Earth emerges while sowing vibrated seeds.

yield more. The action of vibrations can be compared to that of iron's magnetic field. Just as iron atoms react to a magnetic field, seeds, earth and water, human beings react to vibrations. Sahaja Yoga makes it easier to understand how vibrations can be used as a tool to bring positive transformation in plants and animals.

Vibrated water not only enlarges and improves the sprouting potential of non-hybrid seeds, but also activates the plants' growth. Plants treated with vibrated water are greener, more vital and have a significant lead in their growth over non-vibrated ones. Hence, vibrated water can be used to solve many obstacles that currently block our path not only in agriculture but also in the larger domain of the sustenance of the flora and fauna of our planet.

We have to bear in mind that the connecting angle in the water molecule between oxygen and hydrogen is 104.5°. This angle is very stable and does not change under the influence of physical experiments of pressure, temperature and the like. The capacity of this angle is to dissolve various chemicals in the water. As vibrations are a living thing, through the action of vibrations on water molecules, this connecting angle gets changed to improve the dissolving capacity of water, positively and negatively for chemical substances.

With the practice of Sahaja Yoga, we experience that as the vibrations flow through the chakras, the body temperature cools down. If vibrations have the same effect on water, then water should also cool down when vibrations are applied to it. It is well-known that cool water has more capacity to dissolve oxygen than warm water. Thus, extra oxygen at the roots of plants enables better plant growth.

Every atom spins at a certain speed and within a certain

distance from each other. Likewise, every atom in water spins at a certain speed and within a certain distance from each other.

Advanced study in vibrated water on non-hybrid seeds by Dr Hamid Mylany in Vienna, Austria, revealed that the action of vibrations on water changes the speed of the atoms' spin and brings the atoms nearer to each other:

> That means that the connecting angle within the water molecule remains unchanged, but a strong, negative field is created through the nearing of oxygen to hydrogen, which in turn gives water the capacity to dissolve (normally undissolvable) elements such as NH_4 and other nitrogen-containing elements. This is the reason why vibrations given to plants bring a nice green colour. As we know from many experiments, the nitrogen gives plants the dark-green colour the more it is applied.

In the first experiment, Dr Hamid treated non-hybrid sunflower seeds with vibrations. The sprouting ratio of sunflowers rates is normally 75–80 per cent. When vibrated water was used, the ratio was increased to 95–100 per cent. Because of the high germination ratio and the strong growth of the plants in the vibrated part of the test area, there arose a severe competition for space, water and light. Such strong competition normally inhibits the growth of plants, but despite the mentioned density in the vibrated area, its harvest was 20–25 per cent better than the control plots.

By this unique method, both crops and livestock saw an increased yield. Research at the Mahatma Phule Krishi Vidyapeeth Rahuri University in Maharashtra revealed that as cows were exposed to vibrations, they became healthier and yielded more milk.

More recently, Sahaja Yoga and the Indian Council of Agricultural Research (ICAR), New Delhi, conducted experiments in 10 national research centres spread over three states viz. Andhra Pradesh, Maharashtra and Rajasthan. A full agricultural season was spent conducting these experiments on various field crops and horticultural crops.

Similar experiments were conducted in Dharamshala, Himachal Pradesh. Like humans, animals have chakras as well. As their kundalini is ignited with vibrations, their chakras become dynamic, resulting in better health and improved milk yield.

Similarly, plants respond to positive vibrations. The process is simple and natural, and more production can be achieved in less space.

Here are some of the findings of the Sahaja Yoga treatment of seeds and plants using vibrations:

- Excessive use of chemical fertilizers had made the vibrations of the soil very hot. Excessive heat hampered the organic growth of plants. Sprinkling the soil with vibrated water cooled the vibrations of the plot.
- The seeds' natural immunity was restored by sprinkling the seeds with vibrated water. It enhanced their resistance to insects and pests apart from minimum epidemic conditions.
- The quality of grains, fruits, flowers, vegetables, etc. improved.
- Seed germination rate improved.
- Better crop growth and vigour.
- Increase in milk production in cattle.
- Improvement in the health of livestock.

- Trees that had dried due to acid rain could be revived if they were less than 12 years old.

Sahaja Yoga research enables us to use vibrations to increase agriculture production and opens up the possibilities with the power of Mother Earth. As the kundalini of Mother Earth sprouts the seeds, she also absorbs our negativity. When we walk barefoot on the earth, we can feel a surge of vibrations rise in our chakras. Conversely, if we press the palms of our hands down on the earth, she absorbs the negative vibrations from our chakras and refreshes us. It makes it easier to understand that the intelligence at the tip of the seed is no different than the intelligence at the tip of our Mooladhara Chakra.

19

'BEHOLD THE MOTHER'

The Tao that can be told of
Is not the Absolute Tao;
The Names that can be given
Are not Absolute Names.
The Nameless is the origin of Heaven and earth;
The Named is the Mother of All Things.

—Lao Tzu

Cosmos after cosmos is ceaselessly giving birth. Each cause is a mother—its effect is the child. When the effect is born, it becomes pregnant with a cause and gives birth to the wondrous effect of mother and child. As science deciphers the DNA, perhaps one day, it may learn the secret nexus between the Primordial Mother and Her children. To the one who asked the way, Ramana Maharshi answered, 'Go back the way you came.'

We came from the womb; even before Christ, before the most ancient of scriptures, the memory of the matrix was etched in the universal unconscious as the Primordial Mother—the feminine principle. Recent discoveries in the Son Valley excavations show evidence of Her worship in the

The Pieta by Michelangelo at the Sistine Chapel.

prehistoric Stone Age 30,000 years ago.*

> First there was the sea
> All was dark
> There was no sun, no moon
> No people, no animals, no plants.
> The sea was everywhere
> The sea was the Mother.
> The Mother was not people
> Not anything, nothing at all.
> She was the Spirit
> Of what was to come and
> She was thought
> And memory.
>
> —Kogi mythology, Colombia

Our seeking cannot be complete unless it embraces the full meaning of these truths. More recently, research led by Mark Stoeckle of Rockefeller University, New York and David Thaler of the University of Basel, Switzerland, examined 'big data' insights from the world's fast-growing genetic data basis and found our common ancestor, the Mother who lived 250,000 years ago. It is not surprising that the Mother left resilient genes that are carried by the human race. The findings were made by scientists who surveyed the genetic 'bar code' of five million humans and animals.

Stoeckle observed, 'At a time when humans place so much emphasis on individual and group differences, maybe we

---

*Excavated in 1980 by Prof. J. Desmond Clark of Berkeley and Prof. G.R. Sharma of Allahabad University, Son Valley, District Madhya Pradesh, India.

should spend more time on the ways in which we resemble one another and the rest of the animal kingdom.'

Undoubtedly, we share a common ancestor; however, its activating form, like the Jungian archetype—the Mother Goddess as the source of fertility—is fundamental to our consciousness. While the Hindus worshipped the Mother Goddess as Adi Shakti, the Greeks revered her as Athena. Time and again, the Mother Goddess has had to incarnate to break the barriers of evolutionary ignorance. Many negative forces that obstructed the human quest were collected by the human ignorance and she had to destroy them.

Mother Mary is the continuum of the same recognition. Until the end of the fifteenth century, the Madonna appeared everywhere. The popular movement portrayed the Virgin Mary as the ultimate healer and the quintessence of love, charity and compassion, as one historian described it. Her followers placed the Virgin on a higher emotional plane than the purely masculine Trinity. This new gospel of Mary, carved in every Gothic cathedral, consecrated to 'Our Lady,' swept Western Christendom, compelling the church to sanctify it. Great festivals came into being to celebrate the Virgin's life. Since it posed a threat to the Church, the Church Fathers repeatedly attempted to write her out of history.

As human consciousness moved into more abstract realms of thought, it became attached to the Taoist concept of Yin and Yang, which led to the love imbued in the 'feminine principle'.

The feminine principle deeply inspired artists in their paintings, sculptures and architecture during the European Renaissance. In modern times, the collective rising of the sacred energy of the kundalini ushers a new renaissance in our awareness that outlines the aesthetics of harmony with the feminine principle.

If history repeats in all its aspects, it is possible that the same feminine principle may have again manifested amongst us. Christ implied that he 'will send you a counsellor, a comforter and a redeemer... The Holy Spirit will teach you all things.' Let us explore this possibility in the light of certain indications and predictions in the next chapter.

EPILOGUE

All under heaven have a common beginning.
This beginning is the Mother of the world.
Having known the Mother,
We may proceed to know her children,
We should go back and hold on to the Mother.

—Lao Tzu

In the period of distress, around the year 5,000 BC, Lord Krishna came to uphold dharma. As he stated in the Bhagavad Gita. 'Whenever there is a decline of righteousness and rise of unrighteousness, then I send forth myself,' and indeed, in the age of darkness—2,000 years ago—Christ came forth to save mankind.

He, too, said:

'I will pray to the Father and He will give you another Comforter that He may abide with you forever.'

That the Father does abide within the self-realized as the Eternal Spirit, every self-realized soul can bear witness. Thus, the individual becomes part and parcel of the collective being that is the spiritual reality. This is the connection that is the true baptism, the Dvija or second birth of Hindu philosophy, which Christ also promised and which is described in the Quran as the Day of Resurrection.

> He created you as one soul, and as one soul He will bring you back to life.
>
> —The Quran 31.28

What else is this but the collective consciousness in the Life Eternal?

> On that day we shall seal their mouths—their hands will speak, and their very feet will testify to their misdeeds.
>
> —The Quran 36.63

This is described the as non-verbal language of vibratory awareness, which is transmitted through the subtle sensation in the body extremities.

> The fate of each man we have bound about his neck. On the day of Resurrection we shall confront him with a spread wide open, saying: Here is your book—read it. Enough for you this day that your own soul should call you to account.
>
> —The Quran 17.12

This describes how Kundalini herself records her own history and carries the scars of our self-inflicted injuries.

The manifestation of this spiritual reality, in the modern world, has been foreseen by realized seers and sages since ancient times. Twentieth-century American astrologer and psychic, Jeane Dixon, predicted the birth of the coming avatar (divine incarnation) in about 1924 (Shri Mataji Nirmala Devi was born on 21 March 1923). In England, William Blake prophesied, very clearly, in his poetry about the coming age—where men of God would become prophets empowered to make other prophets (Sahaja Yogis giving realization to the guru principle in others). Many of the places specifically mentioned by Blake have proved to be closely connected with the development of Sahaja Yoga in England, especially the Vale Street of Lambeth, where the first ashram has been established and other localities connected with the various residences of Shri Mataji.

Among all the ancient writers of astrological prediction, the greatest master is Rishi Bhrigu, who lived more than 12,000 years ago. His two great treatises *Bhrigu Samhita* and *Nadi Grantha*, written on leaves of lotus palms, describe the horoscope of man according to the combination and permutations of stars at his birth and the future world events of spiritual significance. In the present day, when so many are seeking the New Age, and so many self-certified teachers and masters are floating enterprises of all kinds to attract the seekers; it would help if we tallied the description given in ancient prophecies against modern reality. Thus, we should be able to recognize the incarnation described by our Lord as the Redeemer, the Counselor and Comforter, who will instruct in all things concerning sin and judgment. Many have predicted that this incarnation will be an expression of the feminine principle, the Holy Spirit of Adi Shakti of the Indian tradition.

These ancient writings are replete with proofs of the advent of Shri Mataji as the saviour of modern times. Her person, her teachings and the Nirmala Vidya, which she teaches, are the fulfilment of these prophecies. The clearest of these indications are contained in Bhrigu's *Nadi Grantha*, which was edited with Marathi commentary by another sage, Bujander, about 300 years ago.

According to *Nadi Grantha*, in 1970, a new transformation in human consciousness will commence (the Sanskrit word used is 'manvantar'). The Vaivastav (period preceding Kali Yuga) and Kali Yuga itself will end. Then man will rule with his Supreme Power (with his Spirit). After the death of a yogi in 1922 (Venkataswami), a great maha yogi will take birth. This maha yogi will be an incarnation of the Holy Ghost and will embody all the divine powers of God (Parabrahma), that is, she will be the one that controls the divine power. That yogi will have the shakti of doing or not doing (kartrumakartrumshakti). In previous ages, seekers of truth had to take to devotion (bhakti), knowledge (gyana), Patanjali Yoga and all such different methods and disciplines, in order to achieve the joy of moksha. Thus, they could achieve fulfilment of their heartfelt duty of life (itikartavya) and hence, get their heart's meaning. In those days, one had to undergo a very severe type of penance in order to awaken the sleeping spiritual energy of the kundalini and to make it ascend through the different subtle centres. But, by the grace of the unprecedented method introduced by the maha yogi, the seekers will be able to achieve the joy of moksha in their own lifetime spontaneously and they will be able to see the rising of the kundalini (in Bujandar's Marathi commentary the phrase is '*hytasa desi, hyatsadola*'). There will be no need to give up the body by adopting a state of samadhi (a method adopted of shutting oneself in a cave and dying there while in meditation). But by the capacity of Yoga, one will even be able to achieve victory over death. There will neither be the need to leave your body nor think of your rebirth. The realized soul through this yoga will not have to worry about food, clothing or shelter. Diseases and mental sicknesses will be completely destroyed, and such people will not need the institutions known as hospitals anymore. They will have a power to develop a subtle body and other powers.

Every one of these predictions is fulfilled in the life work of Shri Mataji Nirmala Devi. She was born at the geographical centre of India in the hill station known as Chhindwara, exactly at noon on 21 March 1923, the day of the spring equinox when day and night are equal. On 5 May 1970, Shri Mataji introduced the method of Sahaja Yoga by which realization is achieved effortlessly and without any penances or fasting on the part of the seeker. The spirit manifests as the witness and man conquers his appetite through detachment.

Thousands have seen the rising of the kundalini and the pulsation in different chakras when Shri Mataji awakens the secret power of the seven centres. Jung spoke of a collective unconscious common to all mankind that he himself had glimpsed through his own dreams and insights as well as those of his patients. He also knew and taught that this collective realm is only to be attained by a maturing process of self-realization, casting of illusion and imaginings that hide the collective reality, and hinder its realization into collective consciousness, with the dawning of a new awareness.

Sahaja Yogis know that this describes how the kundalini herself records her own history and carries the scars of our self-inflicted injuries. All this knowledge becomes an open book after self-realization and aids the recovery of the subject.

It is also true that as one establishes one's realization by giving to others, material problems of income, goods and shelter are miraculously solved as well. That is not to say that our senses become numb, on the contrary, we become an instrument of our spirit instead of our ego. The Spirit enjoys herself. She does not seek satisfaction from outside as she herself is the source of contentment. Nor does she remain limited by one's conditioning—she enjoys variety, exuberance and mirth.

This vibratory knowledge is absolute knowledge. Shri Mataji herself never consulted any books, but radiated innate knowledge on every subject with astonishing insight and understanding, 'Sahaja Yoga is beyond rationality—it is like the sprouting of a seed into a big tree—you cannot explain it. Now you have to proclaim that this fulfils the ancient prophecies. This is the revelation and testament of modern times.'

This is the advent of the New Age of the Truth. Let us forget whatever hardships we have suffered in our search in the past. It does not matter if some could not find it before. We have to open our minds and understand that though the discovery is unprecedented, it does not make any seeker or predecessor small. If some experiments are made, it does not matter if ultimately, we have found the way. It is a collective achievement. Perhaps, it was to happen in the chaos of modern times, and many who have been earnestly searching it in many lives are reborn to have their promises fulfilled. Maybe we were our predecessors. The seeker has to now confront himself honestly and with the strength of truth, to break away from the past conditioning, to find fulfilment of his spirit. Sahaja also implies that it is inborn. We all have the same potential to become the Spirit, and now, the time has come to transform this potential into a living reality. It is a direct and pragmatic approach. It rejects any kind of games or power trips. It denounces rigidity, fanaticism, asceticism or any ism. Each individual must respect himself and earn his own living, never be a parasite on others or society. Marriage is a sacred institution, necessary for both individual growths and as the foundation of society. Children born of spiritual parents will be the great souls of the golden age. The Mother has prepared the feast for her children, and we are to enjoy it and celebrate.

All the great incarnations are respected and their essence respected. However, rigid adherence to a particular one eclipses the integrated understanding of the Divine. Each incarnation illuminated a certain aspect of the Divine and added a stepping-stone for human ascent. Hence, to hold on to one or other stepping stone is to live on an isolated island. The Divine can only be experienced in the collective consciousness, and there is no space for individual notions, sects, creeds or ego.

In the process of collective evolution, what one discovers also works out for others. One individual can open the door for others. As a certain number of people of a particular ideology of permutations and combinations got their realization, the rate of realization increased rapidly. As the rate of self-realization gains momentum, no books need be mastered, no sermons need be learnt, no alms need be given, no mountains need be scaled, no initiations need be taken—it is all simply Sahaja: ours spontaneously. The fruition time has come and the Mother gives it to all her children with love, joy and compassion:

> Holy Spirit will come upon thee
> And the power of the most high
> Will enlighten thee.

Yes, life has its woes, its ups and downs. There is misery, suffering and repulsion. But if we also become miserable, then only misery is perpetuated. Let us transcend the limits of our environment with the positive energy of our kundalini. As she pierces the seventh chakra, the Sahasrara feels like a child sucking the joy from the Universal Mother. The joy rivets like waves to distant shores and returns with much greater force. When our joy reaches the joy of others, the ripples return and make a beautiful pattern of our world.

Thus, as we pour the love of Mother Kundalini to sprout the kundalinis of others, the love comes back to us a thousandfold. Every sprout was a seed someday; likewise, every winner was a beginner someday. After all, one has to start someday!

As we take the first step, we will see the seed sprouting in front of our eyes. Not long after, the shoot will grow into a big tree that will provide shade and fruits to the weary traveller. Not just that, the weary traveller will no more journey alone in his mind, but will be joined by his Spirit. With the blessings of the Spirit, the whole universe would befriend him. Moreover, the blind will see with the eyes of the mute and the deaf will hear with the ears of the blind. For sure, by befriending the Spirit, our journey will become sweeter and shorter!

Interestingly, this corresponds to the vision of the tenth-century prophet, John of Jerusalem:

> When the millennium that comes after this millennium ends, men will have finally opened their eyes. They will no longer be imprisoned in their head and in their cities, but will be able to see from one end of the earth to another and understand each other. They will know that what makes one suffer hurts another. Men will form one huge

body of which each one will be a tiny part. There will be a common language spoken by everybody and thus, finally, a glorious humanity will come into existence.*

As the kundalini penetrates all the aspects of our daily life, art, culture, music, economy, agriculture, science and politics, the prophecy of the glorious age will unravel. The human being is the masterpiece of the Divine artist. Hence, this precious work of art is to be adorned—it is not for aggression or escape, but for celebration and glorification of our spirit as envisaged by Leo Tolstoy: 'There is something in the human spirit that will survive and prevail, there is a tiny and brilliant light burning in the heart of man that will not go out no matter how dark the world becomes.'

---

*John of Jerusalem was born in 1042 near the Benedictine Monastery of Vezelay, France, where he himself became a monk. With eight other knights he founded the order of the Knights Templar in 1119 and wrote the book of prophecies. The book was rediscovered only recently as a fourteenth-century manuscript in the Monastry of Sagorsk, near Moscow, as part of the KGB archives. It is now available as *Le Livre des Prophesi*, Jean-Claude Lattes edition, 1994.

www.ingramcontent.com/pod-product-compliance
Lightning Source LLC
Chambersburg PA
CBHW020852160426
43192CB00007B/885